CREDIT SCORE

Know How to Repair Your Credit Score Using Tried

(How to Repair & Improve Credit Score and Increase Business Credit)

Adam Pollack

Published By Phil Dawson

Adam Pollack

All Rights Reserved

Credit Score: Know How to Repair Your Credit Score Using Tried (How to Repair & Improve Credit Score and Increase Business Credit)

ISBN 978-1-77485-311-5

Published By Phil Dawson

ISBN 978-1-77485-311-5

Legal & Disclaimer

The information contained in this book is not designed to replace or take the place of any form of medicine or professional medical advice. The information in this book has been provided for educational and entertainment purposes only.

The information contained in this book has been compiled from sources deemed reliable, and it is accurate to the best of the Author's knowledge; however, the Author cannot guarantee its accuracy and validity and cannot be held liable for any errors or omissions. Changes are periodically made to this book. You must consult your doctor or get professional medical advice before using any of the suggested remedies, techniques, or information in this book.

TABLE OF CONTENTS

INTRODUCTION.. 1

CHAPTER 1: THE FAIR CREDIT REPORTING ACT 2

CHAPTER 2: WHAT TO REPAIR YOUR CREDIT SCORE A
STEP-BY-STEP PLAN TO HELP YOU IMPROVE YOUR CREDIT.
.... 11

CHAPTER 3: BUILDING BUSINESS CREDIT......................... 21

CHAPTER 4: BUILD IT YOURSELF CREDIT BUILDING.......... 31

CHAPTER 5: I'M IN POOR CREDIT. NOW, WHAT?............. 40

CHAPTER 6: WHAT THE CREDIT SYSTEM WORKS 46

CHAPTER 7: UNDERSTANDING THE SYSTEM 67

CHAPTER 8: CAUSES THAT CAUSE CREDIT FAILURE CREDIT
.... 74

CHAPTER 9: BEWARE OF YOUR LIMITS 80

CHAPTER 10: WHAT IS THE BEST WAY TO REVIEW YOUR
CREDIT REPORT TO FIND INCORRECT INFORMATION? 85

CHAPTER 11: RESOLVING POOR CREDIT WITH GOOD
CREDIT 94

CHAPTER 12: WHAT'S YOUR CREDIT SCORE?................. 102

CHAPTER 13: YOUR CREDIT REPORT.............................. 110

CHAPTER 14: YOUR CREDIT REPORT.............................. 118

CHAPTER 15: AVOIDING GETTING YOUR CREDIT REPORT SINCE IT WILL AFFECT YOUR CREDIT SCORE................... 132

CHAPTER 16: UNDERSTANDING THE LAWS.................... 141

CHAPTER 17: STUDENT LOANS EXPLAINED.................... 146

CHAPTER 18: CREDIT & CREDIT REPORTS 154

CHAPTER 19: HOW TO ESTABLISH YOUR CREDIT 167

CHAPTER 20: UNDERSTANDING YOUR CREDIT REPORT . 173

CHAPTER 21: PAYING BILLS 179

CONCLUSION.. 184

Introduction

The book includes all the tested and effective methods that you can apply to learn about your credit score. Additionally, it includes some useful techniques and methods to figure out how to repair your credit score. In this book, readers will discover how to improve your credit score! This will allow you to be able to live in the home you've always wanted to live in!

Learn about the many strategies you could utilize to improve your credit without paying third-party companies. It is also possible to learn about the process of reading your credit report and the best way to efficiently understand your credit report as well.

Chapter 1: The Fair Credit Reporting

Act

As consumers You have rights regarding the information the credit bureaus provide regarding your creditworthiness and payment history. You are able to remove any negative information from your credit report with the rights provided to you under the Fair Credit Reporting Act.

In the pages to follow, a large portion of the negative information that appears on your credit report can be challenged , or even deleted if you doubt the validity or accuracy of the data. Furthermore, a lot of the negative entries that appear on your credit report have to be removed within a specified period of time.

The Fair Credit Reporting Act is an Federal Law passed by the United States Congress and puts certain limitations and obligations upon credit report agencies. The Federal Law gives consumers specific rights to ensure the highest accuracy of information in their credit report. It aims to make sure that credit reporting agencies (credit bureaus) perform their duties fairly.

Understanding the relationship between Credit Reports as well as Credit Scores

Your credit report as well as your credit score are two of the primary ways that creditors and lenders decide on the creditworthiness of you.

If you are applying for an account with a credit card or loan or credit card, your credit score or credit report (or both) will be checked to determine whether you have a record of insufficient payment on your accounts.

Mortgage lenders review your credit report for previous loan defaults. Credit reports help take a variety of crucial choices that extend beyond the ability of you to get credit cards or loans. This includes leasing an apartment, getting insurance, or seeking work. The utility company also checks on your credit history and score prior to allowing you to use their electric service. You should be sure that your credit report is accurate and current.

Credit Report

Your credit history , including credit cards, loans, collections, medical bills etc. It is all compiled into a single report known as your credit score.

As your report card records your academic performance A credit report measures your ability to manage finances in a responsible way. In the moment, you may be more worried about the marks on your report card, however your financial habits may be a factor in your credit score when you are an adult.

Credit reports are an accounting of your financial transactions or credit history. It's a thorough overview of your payment history as well as the state of your credit accounts. It records who you owed and how much and the amount you paid, and most importantly, how well you paid your bills.

While every company's credit report might appear different, they all share the same fundamental information about the credit activity of your company:

The first part contains details that can be used for identification: your full name, address at present previously resided at Social Security number, birthday date, your profession, your employer's name and address and your marital background.

The next step is the section on credit history. This contains information regarding your credit history including your mortgages, auto loans and credit card accounts as well as student loan. It could also contain the conditions that you have with your credit. It will also include the much you owe to your creditors, and the payment history. It will include the names of the creditors as well as the number of their credit accounts as well as the subscriber's number, the type or nature for each credit account the date of each account's opening as well as the credit limits of the accounts, the balance that is outstanding and the current status of each account and your payment schedule for the month.

Your credit report can also give details about any bankruptcy that you've filed, the judgments you have received from the courts or whether you've tax lien on your property.

The next section contains information about inquiries regarding your report. The report lists institutions, businesses or individuals who have recently looked over your credit report. If you make an application for credit and sign your application, you're authorizing the creditor to look into your financial records.

There's a part of the report about which most people aren't even aware of. It is referred to by"the "consumer declaration." It permits you to give explanations or arguments of up to one hundred words length on items in the report that you are not in agreement with.

Examine your credit reports each year to ensure that there aren't any errors - particularly before you make major purchases like the purchase of a house or car in which case you'll need to get an loan.

Credit Score

The data in your credit report could be converted into a numerical number known as the credit score. It summarizes your credit history and assists lenders in determining how likely you'll repay a loan , and also pay them when they are due.

Your personal financial transactions in your credit report reveal your borrowing history and credit scores are an amount that represents your creditworthiness.

If you are applying to borrow money, the lenders need to know the risk they will take when they lend you money. Your credit score provides them with an impression of your creditworthiness at the time they review it. It can affect whether you are eligible for new credit as well as the terms, which include the interest rate that banks offer you. The score of your credit card changes with time as your financial situation alters.

The score ranges from 300-850 and the higher score indicating less risk to the lender. In general the case of credit scores, one with 680 or higher is thought to be excellent.

The most well-known scoring credit is called that of the FICO score, which is named after the Fair Isaac Corporation, the firm that was credited with creating the score.

They also employ the same credit score when they offer various types of loans. If the information that you provide in your credit reports from all three credit agencies are different the credit score you receive from each agency will differ.

How Do Credit Scores Are Calculated?

The more you understand about the way your credit score is calculated more you know about how it's calculated, the easier it gets to increase your score and build up good credit. A higher score on your credit means you are much more likely be accepted, as well as with lower interest rates.

Credit scores are calculated on five components that each carry a different weight in the overall calculation.

Let's begin by taking an overview of how computers determine your score and the weight that is assigned in each class. The following percentages are calculated based on the five categories of those who are part of the population.

35% - History of Payment

It's a simple document that shows whether you've made your payments in full. We all know that late payments can be detrimental. Collections, charges, bankruptcy, foreclosures and judgments are all in this category.

30% - The Amount Due

This examines the "utilization ratio" that is how much you're using out of the credit that you're able to access. The lenders believe that those who are near the limit of their credit will be more likely default on payments. Ideally, you should maintain your balance at 30% to 35% of your limit.

15 Percent - Credit History History

The amount is determined by average time since your accounts were opened and the length of time since the accounts were last used. The longer you've been in possession of an account that has good credit history it is more likely that you'll continue to pay your bills promptly.

10 percent - Credit Types

Most scoring models want to have an assortment of different kinds of credit. The ideal scenario is a mortgage and an installment account, like car or student loan, as well as four or five revolving accounts like credit cards. Creditors want to know you are able to manage various kinds of accounts with a sense of responsibility.

10 10% - - Inquiries

This indicates the frequency with which you've created new accounts. Models of credit score don't want seeing a lot of inquiries for different kinds of accounts in a brief period of time. In the event of opening a lot at once, it can hurt your credit score. This typically indicates that you are in financial trouble and looking for cash to help them out of a jam.

Chapter 2: What to Repair Your Credit Score A Step-By-Step Plan To help you improve your credit.

The ability to repair your credit score is always like a fantastic idea because to many , it seems as if it's impossible! Sometimes, that you'd like you could improve the credit score of your score, but you do not know where to begin! It's very easy to tell yourself you'd like to improve your credit, but not take action to make it happen.

What should you do? Where do you begin? Do you have the ability to get your credit back?

In all honesty the answer is yes! It is indeed possible to repair your bad credit, but beginning it could be a challenge, but don't worry, as this is a step-by-step guide that will aid you on the right path to improve your credit score.

This is not a quick solution; it will take time to repair your credit! It usually takes about six months to see any change in your credit or improvement, but it could be more than a year, and you will be able to see a positive change.

1. Make sure you check your Credit Report

The first thing to do is you should examine your credit report thoroughly! It is essential to review every single detail in your credit report. You don't want to miss anything, so make sure you take it over a number of times. You'll hear this phrase over and over but it's a great beginning point to help you to repair your credit. Simply Do It!

2. Check for errors within your Credit Report

In the next step, you must identify all the errors on your credit report, and correct the issues. If you've committed an error when you fail to make a payment, it is your fault. However, don't get caught because of someone else's error. If you discover a error, it is important to keep track of every error , and then put the matter in dispute.

3. Disputing Your Errors

If you are truthful, if there is a dispute over your suspicions of errors this could help in helping you repair certain aspects of your credit. Some disputes won't be considered, however in the event that you find mistakes that are not correct it is important to rectify them to ensure that you are able to access accurate details about your cred t score.

4. Incomplete Payments - Catch Up with them

If you realize that you have debts you aren't paying on, or have actually been late on payments several times You must make them pay right now! It is imperative to make up any payments that you might have missed, so that your history of payments will be significantly improved.

5. Reduced Payments

In truth the truth is that some payments can be very expensive. But, if you reach out to your lenders or creditors and ask them to cut the amount of payments per month and help in repaying the amount owed. Rememberthat lenders will want your money , even if that takes a few months before they can get the entire amount. But, they still receive their money back, so they'll be content.

Contact the lender to ask to reduce your monthly payments. This could be beneficial to your credit and you as it allows you to establish good repayment history. When you repay the loan and improve your credit score significantly.

It's a very stressful step. Don't give up! You could be on the 24/7 on the phone. I prefer to think of it as negotiation or trying to negotiate the most competitive price for the item. Each phone call that you make can save thousands of dollars. Keep that in mind. The money you save from this bill can be used to pay off another bill, and so on.

6. Do not be apprehensive about repayments, Call A Credit Agency

If you're in the bottom of your finances and don't have enough money to pay off all your debts You can talk to a credit company. There are many agencies that can assist you in consolidating all of your debts into a single monthly payment.

This will not only assist you eliminate the debt, but help to make your monthly payments less and more feasible.

(I do not endorse this. When you can perform this yourself in the 5th step Why should you give someone else the money you don't have! If you really don't have the time to handle all the phone calls , and that's an alternative.)

7. Make Payments on Every Bill and Make Payments On Time Each Month

The most important thing to do to ensure your credit score improves is to pay each and each month's installments in time. Don't forget to pay any bills for utilities and keep track of your rent, as well as any other expense you incur.

If you continue to make each installment, you'll be able to discover that you will establish a solid payment history. This will help improve your credit score. Also, to ensure that you don't forget any payments, create an automatic standing order. These are when the payments are taken automatically from your account and transferred to the company each time they are due for payment.

If you're paying the businesses, you should check your statement every month. You don't want to pay more than you should, particularly in the event that you have other bills to think about. It is important to have a decent lifestyle every month, so make sure the proper amount is paid out each month.

8. You may be able to get a late Payment wiped off of your Credit

If you've made some unpaid payments, in past you might be able to have those taken off your credit history. Based on how great the relationship you have with a company could be, and how great your personal habits are and how well they work together, they might be able to take the late payment notice from your credit report.

If you're looking to give it a go then why not approach the business in writing and inquire if it could be feasible. Eliminating any late payment could be a fantastic option to boost your credit overall.

Furthermore when you have one late payment wiped out from each company you've worked with, all of it will add up to a better credit score.

9. Use a Secure Credit Card

When you hear the words credit card being mentioned, you might feel a bit scared because you immediately believe it is a reference to the risk of a credit card. However secured credit card is a bit different than a regular credit card.

In the beginning you must put money into your account in the account to make use of this feature to make sure you do not pay more than you are able to afford and don't have a balance at the close every month! But, it could be a fantastic opportunity to get started on building credit. Credit allows you to build credit score. This may appear odd but it's the truth.

This is why you should to make an effort to build an appropriate credit card. But secured credit cards could be a viable alternative if you utilize it properly.

10. Upgrade to an Unsecured Card

After you've made several steady month of payments using secured cards then you can try an unsecure card. This could be a method to improve your credit score even though it is not necessary to select the credit card or you could use a store card.

The use of a department store card - even just one - can be an excellent opportunity to increase your credit score. But, you still have to pay each bill every month to ensure an excellent credit history.

11. You are able to try a Credit Card

You can opt for the standard credit card to improve your credit score. But, don't attempt to apply for multiple credit cards at the same time. Use only one card and create small amounts to be able to pay every month. Even if you only pay fifty dollars worth of items every month, ensure that you pay each month as it will be a huge step towards improving your credit. (At minimum, you should make the minimum payment and don't fall into that trap as well. Make the payment as quickly as you can when you are able!)

12. Don't close a credit card

If you have credit cards from the past however, you haven't used them in quite a while make sure you don't keep them on hand. Although you may not utilize all three credit cards, you don't have to spend more than you should on these.

It is easy to charge a small amount on each one to keep the accounts open. When the month is over, you can close the account. month make sure you pay the balance and repeat the process for the following month. Naturally, you don't have to make purchases for to keep the account in good standing, but you can make your money into the cards that you typically use to purchase. This could be fuel for your vehicle or a meal at a restaurant or an item at the local shop. The key is to choose small as is how much you can spend!

13. Make sure that new loan applications are short and sweet

Finding a loan that will last for months isn't an ideal thing. If you are forced to take out a loan, you should make an effort to locate one within the next couple of weeks. Don't have multiple applicants at one time as it could damage your credit. Instead, pick one and only apply for one you are confident you will be able to qualify for.

14. Do not sign for others while trying to repair your credit

While co-signing on a new car for your boyfriend , or friend may sound appealing however, it can harm your credit. It's not feasible to pay for co-signing a loan on your credit since it puts you in charge of the loan. If it is not paidoff, you're responsible for the debt. It means that you're the one to suffer the credit report that's bad!

15. Build Your Credit

Resolving credit problems is easy, but only if you can build a new credit score that is good and reliable. Yes, it is necessary to fix poor credit, but you should ensure that you build new credit too.

Chapter 3: Building Business Credit

Around 45 percent of small-scale businesses that are denied loans have poor credit as per the Federal Reserve Banks of Philadelphia, Cleveland, Atlanta and New York. A strong credit profile for your company doesn't only allow you to obtain an loan, but it will aid your company to gain new customers. The reason is that, in contrast your personal credit score, any potential supplier as well as partners and customers will access the credit profile of your company anytime. In light of this it is obvious that if you have an unprofidential business it is important to make every effort to improve your credit score in the shortest time possible and to keep it in good shape and free of any traces.

Check your score regularly If you're already acquainted by Equifax and Experian but in order to keep an eye on your company's credit score, you're likely to have to be familiar with Dun &

Bradstreet credit bureau. Although the process of determining your personal credit score is fairly simple the three bureaus employ different methods of determining the scores of business credit as and also asking different lenders for various kinds of information. This can work for your benefit, but because Dun & Bradstreet lets business owners change their basic business information and upload financial information. Complete portfolios that are more comprehensive are actually improving credit scores overall.

Create trade lines: If that you purchase products from third-party suppliers making purchases correctly can increase your credit score for your business. If you've been working with a particular vendor for a long time It is probable that they'd be willing to give you credit on trades for the items you buy frequently. Trade credit is simply the term used to mean that you'll be able to make payments for an amount that is predetermined or perhaps just a few days, once you've received the most recent shipment of merchandise. After you've established this type of partnership, it's then simple to ask your supplier to submit your payments to the credit bureaus that are relevant to you.

It is recommended to strive to create at minimum three of these kinds of relationships because doing this will give you what's called a Paydex score from Dun & Bradstreet which is an indication of your overall track record of payments. Even if you establish relations with smaller suppliers that don't usually report information when they are listed to your credit card as references to trade, the bureau will connect with them and calculate your score.

Pay on time Like the personal financial situation, making payments to creditors promptly is an essential element of building your business's credit in a successful way. If you're looking to obtain the highest Paydex rating at Dun & Bradstreet you are likely to have to do more than pay your bills on time regardless of the reason. Also, the longer you have a credit history is, the better. Hence, the earlier you begin making these connections, the better in terms of your rating.

Make sure you borrow from the right lenders: While taking out the ability to pay back a loan in time will help improve your company's credit score, this can only be true when the lender you choose is reported to the bureaus, which is not guaranteed. Make sure you do your research and sure your financial accountability is helping in every way possible when you do receive the loan. The majority of banks submit their information to the bureaus, and so do online lenders like BlueVine, Kabbage, Funding Circle Fundation,

Lending Club and OnDeck. Fundbox, Lighter Captial, SmarBiz and the majority of cash advance providers for merchants don't. If you're using credit cards for business try to maintain your credit utilization below 20 percent for most effective outcomes.

Take note of public information: Much like your credit report for your business your public records could be viewed by anyone, so you're likely to need to make sure you stay within the bounds of the law. In addition to having the negative public records impact your credit score as a business but they can impact how the general public perceives your company in addition.
Stop collecting as fast as you can.

It is likely to be the best option to address creditors right away rather than wait for the debt to reach collections, should it arrive at this point, it is crucial to remember that you have choices due to what is referred to by the Fair Debt Collection Practices act.
Get the specifics in writing: Within five days of contacting the debt collector is legally bound to give you an email stating the amount you owe, the person you owe it to , and how you can dispute the demand. The majority of debt collectors don't perform this task automatically,

however this means that the first conversation that you make with them should include requesting the information you need and nothing else. The aim for the collector to press the customer to verify that they are willing to pay the debt or pay the amount without having all the relevant information before you could cause you to make a mistake and waive a lot of your rights without realizing that you did it. In addition, requesting an account of the information will stop them from contacting them again until you've received them, which gives you time to put your defenses in order If you've been caught out.

Contest the claim: Once you've received the particulars of the claim in writing the next thing you're likely to do is dispute the claim by using the strategies that were discussed in the previous chapters regardless of whether you believe that you owe the amount in the dispute. This puts the burden upon an agency that collects debts confirm the amount owed and isn't an assurance even for debts that you have to pay. You have 30 days to mail this letter starting from the day you got the information, so the use of certified mail is essential. Make sure you request an acknowledgement of delivery as 90% of the time, the collections agency will refuse to acknowledge that they have received your request. After you have sent this letter and inform the agency collecting the debt of this the agency is not able to contact you until the debt is confirmed. They must also end all reporting and you must insist on this in your letter.

Be aware all of your activities: As mentioned in the past the debt collectors have a limited scope in the ways they can interact with you. However, in many instances, they will attempt to override these limitations as far as they can to convince you for the payment of the loan or agree to the payment arrangement. It is recommended that you keep a detailed record of each time you talk to them. Keep any information they give you so that you can review it to see if there are any violations in the future.

Illegal acts that are not covered previously are speaking to someone other than you or your representative about the debt, making use of inappropriate language, misrepresenting the amount of debt, or making false claims regarding legal action, taking properties or securing wages if they don't plan to take action. If they engage in any of these and they do, then the question of the amount that you owe is essentially irrelevant as you'll be able to pursue actions against them, and even the possibility of taking legal action could be enough to convince them to be able to settle the majority or even all of your debt. Make sure you do not declare that you're taking note of conversations since this could make them appear to be in good spirits and limit your ability to leverage.

Try to keep your words as minimal as you can The debt collector does is for the sole purpose of pursuing the debt so the less you speak the less evidence they will have to apply against you. Be aware that regardless of what they claim in front of you they're not your friend. Nor do they are truly interested in your best interests at heart. They earn commissions that means that the more they receive from you, the more money they make. Do not sign anything and never accept that you are liable for the amount you are owed Be sure to inform them that you're considering bankruptcy and talk about options for payment only if you plan to keep your word. If they decide that you're unlikely to make the payment, and the amount due is less than $2500, the bank might decide to give up and see you as more trouble than you're worth. The debt will stay visible on your credit record for seven years may be worth it, based on your financial situation at the moment.

Be aware of the time limitations After you have received the information provided by the collector agency you'll need to determine the period within in which they will pay the debt, based on the location you reside in (between 3 and 6 years, in the majority of instances). After this time is over, they are unable to longer pursue legal actions against you. It is crucial to know these restrictions because if you make a payment within this time frame Some states permit the clock to be reset. This can be done for acknowledging that the debt you owe or when you sign up for a repayment program.

Chapter 4: Build It Yourself Credit

Building

You can take things to your own.

I talked about the secured credit card in my book. It is the ideal companion of someone who is unable to be accepted for a conventional unsecured account. This kind of card referred to as secured because the institution that opens the account typically a credit union, needs that you open a type of savings account and pay at least $300-500 dollars. If you don't have this amount at the time, you can increase the account until you have reached the amount.

The financial institution will allow you to access credit that is equal to the amount saved in the savings account. This is a credit-card that is not a debit card or prepaid credit card, and it will be reported to credit agencies as a revolving accounts similar to any other credit card. Revolving accounts could make or ruin your credit score because every month you're given the possibility of maintaining an acceptable credit utilization or have a lower credit utilization. It is the percentage of credit available that is being utilized.

In the example above that, if you've got an amount of $500, you'll use $400 of your balance in the course of the month, however, you pay $300 toward that balance before the day that the creditor reports the balance of your account to credit bureaus. your credit utilization would be $100 of the $500 or 20 percent. In the next month, if your balance due on the credit card was $50. Your credit utilization for the month will be 10 percent. As a general rule it is recommended that the credit utilization ratio on your Revolving accounts to be not greater than 33% per month. The best approach is to settle your the balance of your credit card that is revolving to zero each month when you can, in order to keep your credit utilization lower and to keep interest costs at bay.

Credit utilization is one of the calculation that determines 30 percent of the score. Think about the situation this way, when you have a credit limitation of $500 with an outstanding balance of $100, you've got $400 available to you on credit that you do not use, which means the credit scoring system, which is based on computer formula considers you to be better suited to borrowing more money. Thus your score will increase because you keep your credit utilization lower month-to-month. In contrast, if you're on the limit of $500 but consistently are being reported as owing $450, it makes you more an enticement to someone who wants to lend you more money since you're living off credit. This could reduce your score month after month.

Another kind of credit card is the installment account. Examples include a car loan or student loan mortgage. You can also start the installment loans account that is similar to a secured credit card to improve your score. This is how it works is that your financial institution will provide the borrower with money, typically $1,000 , and then deposits the cash in a savings account that is available to you. You then return the loan in the course of a specified number of months. When you have paid the loan in full, you are able to access the the savings account and accrue valuable points, which help to you to reach your desired level.

Installment accounts make a predetermined monthly payment and have a balance of zero once all installment payments are made. For instance, if in order to settle an automobile, you'll need to pay 48 installments of $300, the loan is paid off after the installment payments are made in installments of $300 each month. Revolving accounts, on the other hand might have a different installment amount per month, based on the balance.

The benefits of becoming an authorized user include advantages

One issue I encountered frequently while being a homeownership counselor was people who have no credit history, but are finding it difficult to obtain an mortgage loan. One way to quickly make it appear as though you've got credit score is by having somebody add your account as an approved user. The process of becoming the authorized user can be a relatively risk free method to build an credit history and begin building a credit score. Credit card companies and banks generally report the activities associated with shared accounts on the credit reports of all cardholders.

The primary cardholder is able to do this by simple phone to. After the account information has made its way into your credit reports, you will see a record is established. In some instances it could add many years of credit on your credit report. Be cautious with this method. Be sure to know exactly how your bank account should be disclosed. Find out if you are accountable in the event that the account holder is unable to make a payment, or falls into default or in default. The amount of liability will differ based on the creditor as well as should you decide to create an account jointly owned.

The best option is to be an authorized user for long enough to see the effect you require for your score, and then establishing or reestablishing yourself, and then create your own accounts. You will then be removed from accounts in which you're not the primary cardholder. In essence the authorized user method is used by parents who wish to assist their children to build credit. If your parent has a good credit and has healthy spending habits, you might decide to ask them to include you in their approved user list.

Framework to aid in dealing with debt, budgets and debt

The need for higher financial literacy and credit scores isn't just a concern for families with low incomes, however, it is also a problem for those who are middle class. Four out of four households that earn between $56,113 and $91,356 has lower than 3 months' worth of expenditures saved. Being able to modify your score on credit is something however, having a strong grip on your finances is an additional. It is crucial to begin today to set up an emergency savings plan.

This is a task that requires discipline and a clear motive as to for why that having an emergency savings account is crucial. If you do not have enough money to set up an emergency savings plan today it's your responsibility to come up with a creative way to you increase income for your family. The power of knowledge is definitely there but applying knowledge to enable you to attain a certain goal is the only real power.

If you're among many millions of Americans with a poor credit score, be open about your outstanding debts. Make a list of all the outstanding debts you owe by adding your debts to all creditors. Ask yourself some tough questions regarding finances to discover the reasons you are facing financial difficulties. If you have credit cards, you should decide the number of credit cards you actually require. Think about consolidating your credit card bill. It is possible to do this by contacting your credit card companies.

In order to reduce debt and pay off debt should be an ongoing goal in your life to allow it to be a reality and to be able to act in a manner that is consistent with it. It starts with a concept, which will help you set specific goal with a clearly defined beginning and clear conclusion. To guide your journey, create or modify a family budget and adhere to it within your specified timeframe. Begin paying cash for every purchase If you are able to. Set up or maintain savings.

In terms of your bills, make sure to automate them to pay on time by making use of online banks or online payment for bills. I'm sure we don't know the amount of money going to be sitting in your accounts at any one time, but it is important to establish order within your financial life by being accountable. Setting a date for each bill that must be paid using automatic bill pay will allow you to achieve a level of discipline that you may never have encountered prior to. It may be necessary to make changes to your priorities for certain items. In the end, you'll be able look towards the future more clearly. You must be able to envision and believe that there will come a time in the near future when you'll be free from the burden of poor credit.

Chapter 5: I'm in Poor Credit. Now, What?

If you're having trouble getting credit, there are options you can follow to ensure you can get it fixed as fast as you can.

Step One: Ensure the information you provide is correct.

The first step to clean credit is to ensure that your credit report is correct. We start off by requesting a free credit report, from each bureau, by going to www.annualcreditreport.com. The reports are free and are required by Federal law and cannot be considered as an inquiry in your profile. Since you'll get an individual report from each bureau and you'll know which bureau is responsible for what and to whom. Important. Review each report to ensure accuracy and consistency. Does your name appear correctly? Are all your addresses right? Are there duplicate addresses? There are times when the lender will offer their loan to an collection agency and then your debt could be listed multiple times or more. We'll discuss how to correct your details within this section.

Second Step - Repay any negative accounts

The collections and past due charges and tax liens, among others, other negative accounts should be paid off for you to rebuild your credit score. However, not every account should be paid.

Check when the lender most recently made the request to the credit bureau. The usual collection, past due and charge-off account will be on your credit file for seven years. Bankruptcies, tax liens as well as other records that are public will be on your credit report for a period of 10 years. In the event that your bank has listed that your charge was a discharge, but has not updated their information over the last few years, there's the possibility that they will never update the information and therefore ignoring the account could be the most appropriate option. Let sleeping dogs lie. Keep in mind the power of time, and that the older negative feedback is more meaningless they can have on your score.

If your lender has reported negative information on a regular basis or at present, you'll have to take action. The best solution is to contact the lender and ask whether they're willing to take the account off on your credit file in exchange for a payment. This is up to the lender, and they're not obliged to do it. However, it is not a bad idea to inquire, particularly when it's a collection agency. It is also possible to request an offer of a discount, to make a full payment. It's not often that the collection agency is willing to provide you with both the discount as well as the deletion of your credit but those who don't make an effort to ask for it will not receive an offer, so don't hesitate to ask. Be sure to ensure that any agreement you negotiate is made available to you in writing, prior to making any payments. After you've signed the agreement in writing ensure that you comply in your portion of the deal. If you are aware that you aren't going to have money within 15 days, you can negotiate that the payment will be due 30 days after the deal is reached. The entire process is negotiable up to this point.

If your lender has sold an account to a collections agency and both companies report the account, be sure your original lender has proof how the accounts were transferred, and also has the correct date for the transfer. This will prevent duplicate bad credit.

If the information you are looking for has been paid off or is public record, for example, the bankruptcy or tax lien that has been cleared, ensure that the last state of your account is accurate in its status and the date of your profile. If you are a victim of bankruptcy, does it say the discharge date? Do you have the correct date for discharge? Are the accounts discharged as a result of bankruptcy display the date of filing for the bankruptcy as their closing date? Do they show an empty balance? If you were the owner of an unpaid tax lien, does it prove that it was removed (paid to)? Does the date of release accurate? If the account being paid off is a charge-off or collection is the payment date right?

After you have cleaned up your credit score in the maximum extent possible, you must revisit chapter 3 for how to establish your credit profile The steps are similar for reestablishing your credit. However, first you must clean up. It's not a good idea to cook a dessert in the same pan that you cooked stew without washing it thoroughly prior to cooking it. The same is true here.

To get rid of inaccurate information on your credit report Send an DISPUTE request to each bureau in need of corrections. The majority of Bureaus offer a dispute page on their websites, however should you be unable to find the page or prefer to do the task in writing they have their addresses located in chapter 10.

I strongly suggest that all disputes be resolved online by contacting the Bureaus. Requests for written correspondence will require you to provide the social security numbers as well as the date of birth. If the letters go missing through the post, no one can predict what might occur to the information. Dispute requests may also be done thru your account with www.annualcreditreport.com.

Chapter 6: What the Credit System

Works

The credit system is composed of three entities: you, the creditors along with those who run credit bureaus.

*Creditors They are the firms that you can access credit from.

*Credit Bureaus: These are accountable for gathering credit information from both current and past creditors. They before compiling reports, which can then be modeled as credit reports for each credit-worthy consumer. The credit profile is given to lenders to help them make various decisions, including the amount they'll charge for borrowing, and the amount of penalties you must pay if you fail to pay.

If a creditor requires the report of people who have a certain credit score they may then purchase credit reports from the credit bureaus, making it simple to select specific products and services. The bureaus (creditors) will provide you with appealing information on deals that you must purchase.

Subprime credit scores are the most popular selling point for various agency that report on credit. If you have a credit score that is subprime it is likely that you will be receiving a variety of email invitations inviting you to apply for various credit cards. The reason for this is quite simple when you consider that with a subprime credit rating it is likely that you will to be charged higher fees for getting credit. This is simply because lenders will earn more from the credit you have. If you have a good credit score, you're at a low risk, and lenders will are less likely to charge you for accessing credit, meaning that they earn less when they extend your credit. As I said, with poor credit, you could be paying a lot more than someone with excellent credit. In other words lenders are likely to take advantage of people with poor credit, because they are sure that they will earn more money at the end. If you do fail, you're likely to be paying more than someone with excellent credit! Subprime data is popular that the credit bureaus charge higher prices for it. It is extremely sought-after! This could suggest that creditors and credit bureaus do not care about having a good credit rating. If your credit score is low they'll charge you higher fees! Did you know that nearly 90% of the credit report has been shown to be inaccurate, unreliable or incorrect entries?

You now know the reason your credit score is constantly getting worse despite all efforts. The companies involved are there to make money; they'll even disregard when inaccurate entries are included in your credit report. However they've convinced us that their reports are the truth but they aren't even near the truth. In basic terms, these two participants within the credit system can only be made to obey the law to get things in order. They do not care about you having perfect credit since they all make more even if you have poor credit. That's where the process of credit repair is essential.

The credit system is able to take into consideration both negative and positive data on your credit reports. Negative elements like overdrafts, late payments and the many credit accounts that are on your credit report contribute to lowering your score on credit. So, the less items are listed upon your credit reports the better your score.

You probably are aware, there isn't any evidence on your credit report that your score is bad, good, or even average. How do you tell if your credit score is considered good or good, average (subprime) and bad? Next, I'll provide you with the benchmarks lenders employ to determine if your credit score is excellent (perfect) or normal (subprime) and bad.

What is the best or worst part of your credit score?

Credit scores can range between 300-mid 800. Let's look at the different ranges to provide you with a clear idea of where you are.

720 or more

This is considered to be excellent. You will get the highest rates of interest and repayment conditions for loans.

680-719

This is one that is considered to be good

620-679

This is classified as normal (subprime)

580-619

This is regarded as poor. In this situation you are able to receive loans on lender's conditions and will likely to be paying more to get credit. It is impossible to finance autos If your score is below this threshold.

500-579

This is a bad idea. Credit access at this point is expensive. For example, a 30 year mortgage may have a rate of 3% more.

More than 500

The ability to get credit with this credit score is impossible to afford. It is possible that you will not be able to access any kind of credit.

In essence, everyone wants an excellent credit score as it allows us access to credit at a reasonable rate. This is why you should take every step to boost your credit score when you notice any inaccurate or non-verifiable information on the credit reports. Let me go over this more in depth to help you comprehend the need to act immediately to rectify your credit report.

up to 93% of credit reports contain inaccuracy, non-verifiable, or inaccurate entries. This means that an overwhelming majority of credit reports must be disputed since all of these impact your credit score in a negative way. The proportion of doubtful credit reports is so high that everyone should investigate the incorrect, unsubstantiated or incorrect entries. If you don't do this, you'll be forced to learn this the hard way Have you ever read about the horror accounts of people finding out that their credit score was damaged even though they did nothing to cause it to be bad. A lot of people only discover that their credit score is poor after a loan application is denied this simply means that their credit score is actually bad in the present. Do not overlook any entries in your credit score as it could end up damaging your score. For instance, the date you last made an activity on your account may cause a negative impact on your score. Creditors are notoriously known for changing tiny details of credit report just to smudge your score and cost you higher fees. They are operating in the business of making money, so beware!

Don't be silent when you see different creditors that are reporting the same debt numerous times as it makes it appear as if you're sinking even deeper into debt. Don't forget the creditor that reported the same debt with different accounts.

In accordance with laws, lenders are allowed to keep your credit history/information for up to seven years. It's not uncommon to see them keep the information for longer than 10 years. This means that this information will always show up on the credit reports of your clients, meaning that it can mess your score from year to year.

So, how do you increase the credit rating of your business? It's true that this will not be possible if you're just waiting for the credit bureaus and lenders to act. You must take action to get your credit score higher.

In reality, it's that the procedure is difficult and difficult to at the very least. If you don't know the process you'll be left with nothing changed. This is why a lot of these businesses are busy trying to convince consumers that they are unable to fix their credit, and continue to smudge the credit report of ours. Even though you're entitled to file a dispute, submitting successfully is an entirely different matter. This book will assist you to learn how to accomplish the task of fixing the credit rating. You must ensure that you use the tried and true strategies which actually result in getting those derogatory elements removed permanently. you don't want everything be restored in 60 days or longer. The first thing to be aware of is how to look over your credit report in order you can spot any negative entries. In order to do this, you must obtain the most current reports.

Where To Get Your Credit Reports

There are three primary methods to obtain your credit report each year (by law, you're entitled to obtain copies of the credit reports from all of the three major credit bureaus). The three credit bureaus don't interact with credit card users directly. Instead, they've collaborated to provide one central location that you can ask for an credit report. They've done it by:

*Having a central website where you can request for instant reports at www.annualcreditreport.com

*Having an toll free number that allows you to dial 1-877-322-8228 for your free report. The report will be delivered in 15 business days.

A central address to which you can apply to receive your free report via mail by downloading the form here and then sending it to the Annual Credit Report Request Service The report will be delivered after 15 working days. It is possible to request the free Annual credit report with all the major credit bureaus at various dates or all at once.

In reality, lots of things happen throughout the year, and your credit report for the year could be a reflection of a damaged score. It is essential to monitor your score each month If you're committed to repairing your credit. This requires a credit monitoring company to be aware of what happens each month. If you're looking for a credit monitoring company make sure you choose one that will give your FICO scores, not FAKO scores as they could differ to your FICO scores. The majority of banks and lending institutions typically make use of the FICO score, so it is important to keep an eye on this score. FAKO is known to provide people with an illusion of security as it is usually more in comparison to FICO. FICO score. It is necessary to pay some money to get this score (about 15 dollars each month).

Note:

In addition to having your credit score information from all the credit reporting agencies you can also apply for the credit report in situations that you believe you've been denied credit in a way that is unfairly. You must notify your agency of an event.

If you have highlighted any errors on your credit report and the credit agencies have confirmed your concerns then you may request new credit reports from them. The report will not count as the annual report you're entitled to. Furthermore, you have a right to ask the agencies that report to provide every organization that has viewed your report within the last six months with a correct copy each.

While this may sound like something that is a good idea, bear in mind I've already mentioned that credit bureaus don't have a stake in your having a great score, so don't fall to believe that they can perform any. There's a lot you can know about your credit report , so that you are able to get rid of the impression that things are not as good as they appear. Every single thing in your credit score has a significance. Certain items could be sufficient to cause a dispute, so make sure you don't miss everything. Let me show you the best way to evaluate your credit scores in the following chapter.

How to interpret Your Credit Score

It is important to examine your credit score to ensure that you are aware of changes on the credit score. This will allow you to act quickly whenever you realize there's a problem.

There are a few things you're likely to uncover when you begin a regular checking of your credit report. There are many things you can discover such as identity theft modifications in the last date of report, double reporting and other irregularities regarding your credit reports. A little practice and experience will allow you to spot any the issues that are easily visible in your credit score.

The structure of the Credit Report

Your credit report comprises four main categories

*Personal data

*Public record information

*Credit card information

*Credit enquiries

Personal Information

It is easy to understand It consists of details as: your name, address Social Security number your current address, birth date as well as employer information, aliases and addresses prior to. If you believe that something in this list is not accurately reported or you do not want to make it public in the public domain, you may challenge the information.

Public records information

This section shows any open legal concerns regarding your account. Information about your financial status, e.g. bankruptcies, liens, garnishments and judgments are included in this.

If you're using an TransUnion report you will be provided with the dates that items are removed from the report.

It is the Credit Information Category

It is the most crucial aspect of the credit history report. It contains information such as all current credit lines that are on your account, credit that you have transferred to a collection agency and the status of accounts you have with various institutions. These could show whether they are open, closed or in the process of being debited (sent to a collection agency) or flagged.

This section is designed to gather all information related to your financial habits. In addition to the information above details, you'll also be able to see:

Account responsibility information The information you provide is relevant to all entities that have control of accounts, along with you.

Your balance on each credit card

The most recent payment

- Past information due

The credit limit you have set

History of your account

The credit report is likely to include separate classes to cover different aspects of the report. In this scenario, the accounts linked to public documents real estate Revolving and installment loans, etc. are listed separately. It is essential to verify each entry in this category to verify the accuracy in all aspects. Check for the creditor's name and dates of opening, as well as the amount due, the balance owed, monthly payments and high balances, etc. Also, you should check to confirm that the status that is displayed is correct. Determine if the account is open, unpaid or in collection, or closed. Simply put in the event that something does not match your information and you are unsure, then challenge it. Be sure to not ignore anything on your credit report if you believe it is incorrect. Check for any information that has to do with late payments in the history of payments within the last 30-60 or even 120 days. It is likely to be easy to locate these as the reports are often accompanied by colors.

Summary of the credit report

The report contains information such as when accounts are opened or closing, property, debt outstanding and debt that is in collections. Do not overlook any detail; try to examine every single item within the report. The aim should be to increase the number of zeros inside the report.

Information

The report also lists the various companies and individuals who have requested your credit report and have viewed it. It could also contain details on the places you have created new accounts, and at the which financial institutions. The section could also include any loans or mortgages you've sought in recent times regardless of whether you did it on your own or as part of a group. The information you provide creditors shows the way you spend money and is essential in the process of processing credit applications. Insufficient inquiries are unsettling for lenders. If you have more than one of these can harm your credit score.

There are two kinds of inquiries that are listed on your credit report.

Hard Enquiries

You must be cautious about how you conduct inquiries about credit since they will result in being recorded on the credit file. While some reporting agencies offer an exception for this and record it as merely shopping indications however, they also set an upper limit on the inquiry's duration. However, you must be careful when looking for the lowest priced credit as certain scoring agencies haven't made this provision. Credit applications can lower your credit score if they are recorded in your credit reports.

Soft inquiry

If a marketing agency has pre-empted the credit eligibility of you the soft inquiry could be recorded. Certain agencies conduct a thorough review of your actions and demonstrate an interest for you to become a prospective client.

Terms to be able to comprehend In Your Credit Report

"Charged off" indicates your creditor lost faith with you and is now giving up. Therefore your debt was given to a collection agency to be dealt with. The transfer usually contains all the details that can aid the collection agency in reaching you. Your credit report is transferred to the collection agency. It is important to remember that any debts you might have paid off following the time they were debited cannot be erased from your credit file. You may have paid them off, yes but that doesn't alter the fact that you were in delinquency on the credit card. The debt will be reflected the credit history of your for seven years.

*Revolving account: It is generally the credit card account. It is a reference to accounts where which pay interest continuously, and offers the option of continuous credit that is revolving. The only requirement is to pay interest on the amount due.

*Installment accounts They are accounts that have fixed payment schedules. They could be credit from financial institutions, with specific agreements on when installments are due and completion dates.

"Open" account is the current one-off credit card that you have in your name when you are preparing the report. The majority of these debts originate by utilities companies.

*Collection account The term "collection account" is used to describe accounts that are in your name which were transferred into the hands of third-party companies, i.e. collection agencies. The account appears as a collection account regardless of whether or not you've paid the debt following the event or not.

Understanding the codes that are used in credit reports

The numerous codes could create confusion, especially in the event that you're not familiar with credit reports. Certain codes could differ slightly, based on the agency reporting. However, the majority of codes are the same. Some of them include:

CURR ACCT applies to all your current accounts in good standing on the date that the credit report was prepared. Good standing is when the accounts are adequately taken care of and that there aren't any gaps, or balances which are past due.

CUR WAS CUR 30-2. This indicates that your account was 30 days overdue but it's current.

PAID: This means that the balance has been paid and is inactive.

The term "CHARGOFF" means that the debt has been handed over to an agency for collection.

COLLECT: This means that your account has become in arrears and is being transferred to a collection agency.

FORECLOS: This is a reference to the foreclosure of property.

BKLIQREQ means it was paid in accordance with sections 7, 11 and 13 in the statute. There are instances where certain debts may be erased by legal methods. The amendments mentioned above point to the specific circumstances that apply to this procedure.

DELINQ 60. The number is a sign that a account is in arrears by 60 days or more.

If you wish to dispute any credit report, it's important to understand the procedure for repairing credit before attempting it.

Don't rush into trying because you could end up causing more harm than good.

Chapter 7: Understanding The System

"An investing in education yields the highest return."
~Benjamin Franklin

To be able to live life to the fullest, we need to understand the systems that run through our lives. Take a look at the beginnings of flight for humans. We've all seen it gigantic multi-winged aircrafts that whirling, bounce and collapsing. Sometimes they'll fly over cliffs until they fell. The early inventors had intelligence, ideas and creativity to the max. They simply did not have a good knowledge about the technology they wanted to tap into which was in this case aeronautics.

Many efforts for improvement in our finances condition are not successful in the same way. It's not because we aren't capable however, we do not fully grasp the system. Our attempts to achieve financial "flight" usually meet the same goals.

The average borrower today from the US:

In the case of credit card holders, the typical household credit card debt is $17,799.

27 77% of families have less than $1000 in savings.

half of household believe they'd be unable to pay for the cost of an unexpected $2,000 bill. (source: creditcards.com)

Another way to look at this is to say that about half of Americans live from paycheck to paycheck, and many are in debt more than they need to carry.

Why?

Many people are without understanding the system of finance and credit as well as the practices of financial management which lead to greater financial independence. In the end, instead of living comfortably within their budget, they go up to the point of destruction in pursuit of a magazine lifestyle. Instead of making plans to create an enlightened life instead, they settle for the precarious state that they've been sucked.

Based on the data revealed, it's clear that the majority of us do not know the best way to prioritize our spending or how to make use of credit. In general we aren't sure what to do with our money in a responsible manner. Without this knowledge, we can leave the overall condition of our financial situation to the hands of fate.

In order to begin gaining control: learn about the system.

We can learn an important lesson from the business world and banking...

An unending source of frustration for many small-scale entrepreneurs is their banks' demand that their credit line be utilized in a specific manner. Banks prefer to see balances "revolve". This means that when money is received, it is used immediately to fund the business. If the company has to borrow more money and again, then it is fine.

The main thing banks are worried about is the'source of repayment'. If a company draws funds from its credit line is usually for a specifically defined purpose to cover the duration between the supply of products and services (and the associated expenses) and the acceptance of the payment.

For instance, if an enterprise sells a shipment of widgets that cost $25,000, but doesn't receive payment in 30 days time, the 30 days gap is an ideal place to use money borrowed from the bank. The bank is secure since it is aware of exactly the source of the loan from. When the money arrives and is added to the account the balance is referred to as'revolving'. Business banking requires the responsible utilization of credit.

The concern about the source of repayment could totally alter the way you pay for your purchases if applied to lending to consumers in the same manner. The likelihood the credit card provider will to advise you to carefully examine how you'll make payments for purchases low.

Outside of the business realm We all get ourselves in trouble because we believe the falsehood that is continuously advertised to us the idea that a credit-card is used to buy things that we do not have cash to pay.

This belief is the primary of all disasters!

It is important to think about credit cards as well as other lines of credit in the same way that a company could. Credit cards are only utilized when we are aware of what they will be paid back. The payment source could be in the bank account you set up to put aside funds for a specific purchase. It could also be an estimated amount to be paid in your next pay check. The money can be derived from a variety of sources, however the most important thing to consider when borrowing is this:

If you aren't sure the source of your money Don't make a purchase!

It's a very simple idea however, it's one that culturally it is a challenge to implement in our daily lives. But it's a crucial element to everything else that is. If you are able to recognize this simple rule and applying it to your life , you are able to make an actual, significant and life-changing transformation.

Alongside learning about how to use credit responsibly We also have to be aware of the specific rules for our credit cards and the general ways in which we are urged to live above our budget.

What are your rates of interest?

What is the amount you have to spend on interest?

Are you paying hidden fees?

What external forces keep us from spending when we shouldn't?

What internal pressures create the similar?

What habits are disempowering and must we break?

Each of these questions will be addressed in the sections that follow. Understanding the answers is vital to changing your financial lifestyle.

Get up!

The problem you face isn't one of ability. It's a test of understanding and dedication.

If you can master the basics of finance and credit contained in this book, and then committing to developing new habits that are credit-friendly and habits, you'll soon be well-positioned to live a life that is your own design!

Tips to help you understand the System:

1. Read this book for the understanding of proper use of credit.

2. Find out the terms and conditions of your credit account. What are the rates? What are your charges? What are your terms of payment?

3. Be aware of the stressors, both internal and external that push us to make purchases when we should not.

4. If you aren't sure the source of your money do not spend it!

Chapter 8: Causes that Cause Credit

Failure Credit

We have reviewed some terms you need to know so you can better understand the credit score. This chapter I'll explain the primary factors that may cause your credit score to be low.

Be aware that these may be only a fraction of the reasons , and there could be many more that could be contributing to your credit score being low. If you can identify and connect to your situation from the list above, it is recommended that you take action immediately to improve your credit score as soon as possible.

Afraid of having too many cards

One of the primary causes of having poor credit is having excessive credit cards. If you have reached your credit limit for a card or due to fearing that you will limit being reached and you are afraid of a max out, you apply for a new one, and then another. In the end, you'll end up with enough cards that you don't be able to identify which one you made which big purchase. In addition, you will get a large amount of debt for your cards and will not being able to pay it fully. The debt will continue to accumulate and will begin to strain your credit report.

Credit cards for closing

The third biggest factor that contributes to bad credit is taking out credit cards that have credit. If you do this and your balance on your account is not reduced, your balance remains, however the credit limit you have set will show as zero dollars. It will appear that you've exceeded the limit of your card and can have a negative impact upon your score. Therefore, without fault of yours, it is likely that you will see a negative mark in your credit report. And it will be reported that you've maxed your card even though you didn't. Since 30 percent of the credit rating is due to your debt, this could help to improve your score.

Credit cards that are maxed out

The second mistake is to limit out your credit cards. If you have a limit that is exceeded this means you've used 100% of your allowance and this will not be an ideal situation for your credit score. It can increase your debt ratio by a significant amount, which isn't an ideal situation for your credit report. Creditors will scrutinize your cards with the maximum limit and ask whether you'll do the same thing with theirs. They won't be able to be able to trust you if they see them you're capable of maxing your limit every month.

Excessive borrowing

If you're the type who borrows money for everything and then your credit score will be very low. Like we said earlier that a poor credit score is negative for you since no one will offer you credit. If they do, they will be granted it at a high interest rate that is not ideal for you. It is possible that you will have to pay an enormous amount of interest, which can be extremely risky for your assets of wealth. It is possible that this kind of borrowing will become an everyday thing for you, but it can detrimental to your credit score and lead you to be in a position of having very poor credit.

Wrong scores

A lot of times lenders and companies that issue credit cards might have incorrectly charged you, or added transactions that you could not have performed. This could cause you to be a victim of a low credit score. The creditor could have committed a mistake that led to an error, and therefore it is essential to review and meticulously scan your credit card statements every one time to be sure that there was no error in the information added. This is also true for the credit bureau. You must examine your credit history frequently to ensure that the record is correct.

Mortgaging

Paying the mortgage off late or delaying payments is a huge risk to your credit score. If you delay paying your mortgage you could see your home closed as well as your score could be extremely low. You won't be able to free your house , and you could be able to lose it. It is possible that you'll have difficulty with mortgages in the future . You may are also having difficulty scoring credit and loans. All of this will eventually result in you having extremely poor credit.

Declaring bankruptcy

Sometimes, you'll be attracted to declare bankruptcy to avoid an issue and ease the burden for yourself. However, declaring bankruptcy can cause a disaster for you credit scores. It will drop to zero, which means that you don't have credit in the first place. No one will consider you for credit in the future due to worry that you will default to make payments. Your poor credit score will render it difficult for you to get credit cards since they aren't willing to take the risk.

Collections

A lot of times, creditors use a third party to recover the debt you have to pay them. This is usually the case with creditors who experienced a negative experience dealing with you previously and don't believe in you as much. When this occurs, it will be reflected the negatives on your credit report since it will be noted that the creditor has had enough of trying to get you to pay and taken the decision to hire an outside company to take over the work for them. It is therefore recommended that you do not have your account referred to collections to avoid having a an unfavorable credit score.

Chapter 9: Beware of Your Limits

"I am not sure if I should pay off my high-interest credit cards, or the high debt-to-availability cards those with lower balances the highest amounts, collections accounts, lawsuits, or shop! Help!!!!! " - Evelyn C.

If you're unsure what credit card is the best option to begin with, I'd suggest to first assess your goals and what options you have to aid in reducing your debt. It is important to consider making payments on installment loans like mortgage, car or student loans could improve your credit score, but not as much as the process of paying off your credit cards, revolving accounts like department store or credit cards. When you have made your decision that you want to pay off your debt, there are a variety of methods that you can use to the repayment of your debt.

Method #1: Take on the High Rate of Interest

This approach, which many experts recommend that you follow by making sure your accounts are paid that have the highest interest rate. Paying off the credit card with the highest percentage of annual interest that has a moderate to high balance can save you much more money than tackling the balance that is low or moderate with a low-interest credit card. Once the debt is cleared, they move on to the credit card with the most interest, and so on. In certain situations, this may be logical, but I am not convinced with this approach as being the most effective. For instance, suppose you have a credit card that has a 500 in the balance, 19.99 APR, and a balance of $1000 on a credit card that has an 14.9 APR of 14.9 percent. The lower balance will pay approximately $100 per year in interest. The account with a higher balance of 14.9% will pay $149 annually. In this case, it makes more sense to pay off the larger balance using the lower percentage of annual interest because it will cost more in interest each year. This leads me to the second method.

Method #2: Attack the Balance. Balance
As I said earlier, one of the ways to increase your credit score is to ensure that your credit accounts fall below 35 percent. Hence in the event that you have revolving credit account which are greater than 35 percent of your total balance, this approach could help you. The experts say that for every $1000 that you have in your account it is recommended to limit your balance to less than $350. So, let's suppose you have four credit card accounts, with all having an amount of $1,000. One has a balance of $600 one has the $400 balance and the last one has a balance of $250. This means that you must pay for all of them, however, you should you should apply the highest amount to the three credit cards that reduce them to less than 35 percent. If you are in this scenario then this approach could be the best option for you. The final option, which is actually the best for me is the strategy of tackling the balances with the lowest values first.

Method 3: Debt stack

When I'm paying off credit card debt I love to make what's known as"debt stacking. I arrange all my credit cards that are revolving from the smallest to the largest with regard to balance. I begin by tackling the account with the lowest balance before moving on to the next in this list until I am at the account with the largest balance. Then, I continue to pay all other accounts, however I pay only the minimum amount and transfer the largest amount of funds to the account I'm trying pay off. After I pay off that first credit card using the amount I made on the prior account to the following one. This will increase the amount of payment on the subsequent account and makes it cleared much faster than it would have been without the debt stacking process. This drastically reduces the amount of time you have to pay and the amount of interest that you be paying for your loan. I've found that I am more successful in paying down my debts when I am able to see the results as quickly as I can. Like I said, this method works best for me. ultimately it is up to us all to do what is best for us in our particular circumstance, but it's good to be aware of the options available to you.

Chapter 10: What is the Best Way to Review Your Credit Report To Find Incorrect Information?

The credit reports that are as reliable as they are however not completely reliable. Credit reports are susceptible to mistakes that could damage the reputation of your credit. No matter how responsible financially the discipline you have exhibited might not reflect upon your credit reports. This is the reason it's crucial to keep an eye on the credit score.

The statistics show that from 1 to 4 of five credit reports contain mistakes. In those figures 5 percent of applicants were rejected applications due to incorrect reports. 10 percent of the applicants who found the errors were able improve score by 50 or more points. While credit agencies are accountable for the production of this report, they are the one responsible for the quality of the report.

An obvious indication of an error on your report is to compare the three reports of the agencies. When your score appears to be different or shows a huge divergence from one report to one report, it means that either three or all three of them have missing information which the other agency is missing.

There are three main causes of errors on the credit file:

1. Data sources
2. Time lapses
3. Fraud
4. Time delays
5. Persona information

The majority of errors don't originate from the credit company itself but from the sources of their information. For instance the bank you use may have missed sending an update to the status to the credit card you have on your account. Although you've paid in full on your credit report there is an outstanding balance that remains.

Another mistake is when the one-time lapse. Note that any history of bad loans, either paid or not are likely to be discovered within seven years. The bankruptcy will appear on your credit report for a period of 10 years. You must ensure that you include the years that you've been unable to pay the debt. If your debt is still on the report after seven years, it is an error on your credit report.

Identity theft is a common occurrence with the many methods for the theft of credit card data. If you do not discover any suspicious transaction on the bank statement the unpaid transactions remain on your credit score.

Additionally, each of the credit agencies have their own cut-off dates for generating their reports. It could be due to incorrect reporting , but of delayed report. One agency could have prepared an account of your latest payment, but another agency will be reporting on the following period.

There may also be mistakes If you've been using various names, like an alias, when you make financial transactions. This can result in credit reports that are divided in that one set of information found in your actual name and another on a different name. The other discrepancies could result from different personal information , like inaccuracies of Social Security numbers or addresses, or changing your name of newlyweds.

Any dispute you have to be properly documented. For instance, if you've made a full payment on a loan , but the report states that you are owed a balance you should submit a copy of your receipt for the full payment. Any communications you make with your financial institution or bank should be in writing and the credit agency will be provided with an original copy of the letter.

If you send your letter via post or email, you should request the return receipt or confirmation that your letter was received. Include the receipt confirmation in your dispute documents. Usually, the creditor is granted 30 days to research and confirm your claim. The creditor is then given 30 days to confirm or deny the claim.

If the creditor fails to reply within the 30 day period of agency's notice, then the account must be removed. If there's a delay in your dispute you can request the credit bureau to add your dispute's statement to your credit record. Although it is your obligation to check the accuracy of your credit reports, it's the credit bureau that is accountable for correcting it.

If you are writing an agreement, it's recommended to include all details. You should be able to identify the exact details of your dispute, such as the item and the amount, as well as the status or any information that is incorrect. Then, you must state your facts and position regarding the dispute. In the end, you should make a request for changes to the credit report by either correcting or deleting the information. Be sure to write professionally and avoid negative, intimidating cr emotionally loaded comments.

Here is an example of the letter of dispute:
[Your Name]

[Your Address]
[Your City, State, Zip Code]
[Date]
Complaint Department
[Company Name]
[Street Address]
[City, State, Zip Code]
Dear Sir or Madame:

The reason I'm writing is that I want to contest the following information that is in my file. I have highlighted the information I am disputing in the copy I have attached from the document I was provided.

This item [identifies item(s) disputable by name of the source, for example tax court or creditors and also identify the kind of item such as judgment, credit card or tax court, etc.This item is inaccurate or insufficient because [describe what is incorrect or incomplete and the reason for it. I'm requesting to have the item removed [or request a different specific modification] to rectify the error.

Included are copies of the [use this sentence , if applicable, and provide any documents, like court documents and payment recordsto support my claim. Re-examine this matterand delete or amendthe item(s) in dispute as soon as you can.

Sincerely,

Your name is

Attachments: [List the items you're enclosing.Enclosures: [List what you are enclosing.

This letter can be found at: http://www.consumer.ftc.gov/articles/0384-sample-letter-disputing-errors-your-credit-report

If you have a complete credit score that's a reflection of your actual credit standing You can reap the benefits of financial discipline.

Credit reports are your score. The higher your score more secure you'll be financially. For instance, you could be approved for a loan quicker based on your credit score. In the past, bankers or other financial institution weeks and even months assess the loan application With credit scores, today they provide a quick gauge for your financial capacity in a timely manner and your financial accountability.

The credit report also makes the loan process more fair as it eliminates any bias that is due to race, gender and marital status, religion, and other personal details. Many lenders have the tendency to judge you based on the financial capability. If you have a credit history they are able to concentrate on the elements that are essential to making you eligible for loans. The credit history of your past can be rehabilitated as you increase your financial accountability. It was previously impossible to do so when an unpaid debt is an inexplicably permanent part of your credit report.

A greater number of loans are possible due to lenders being able to offer an array of options that match your score. Instead of offering a handful of standard items that could be a reason to deny you a loan the lender can alter their offer according to your score, rather than denying you completely. Credit reports allow lenders can reduce the expense of their credit analysis. They are also capable of offer low interest rate. For instance it is the case that United States enjoys lower interest rates than European countries due to the accessibility of credit reports.

Chapter 11: Resolving Poor Credit

with Good Credit

If you're trying to boost your credit score, there are some things you should do. The first step is to bring your credit under control so that you can transform it into excellent credit. Another is to secure more credit that is good. If you have credit cards but they are not being used, this is fantastic. Even if there is an outstanding debt on these cards, they may be used to your benefit. You must ensure that you don't lose the cards.

If you're left with an unpaid balance in your card, make a note of it down. Write down every card that has a balance, as well as how much it is, and the amount that is due. It may be difficult to believe as you examine how much debt you're carrying, but it's crucial to know. Certain of the lesser loans may be able to eliminate in a short time if you consider it. A few of the more significant ones are likely to manage while at the same time.

Take note of your income and the amount of money available to pay for your credit card debts. Are you able to make enough money that you can pay off a couple of smaller debts and leave a few credit cards in the open? If so, excellent. What you need to do is contact the business and negotiate with them. You can offer a lower amount than the amount owed and inform them that should they agree to accept the amount, you will be able to pay them right away. The majority of credit card companies will accept the offer. Even when they offer the card company $100, or lower than the amount actually due, they'll be content with the cash because they are confident that it is at a minimum going to earn them something. However, if they decline, it's impossible to predict whether you'll declare bankruptcy, and then they won't get the money they owe.

In the event of paying off your credit cards, you will result in them being closed because your credit-granting company will remove the card from you once they receive their money. This is why you shouldn't wish to settle every single card you are in debt with. If you take the time to pay the whole amount off, then you'll be losing all of them, and it will cause no new credit appearing on your report. This is likely to harm you more than it will aid you. It might seem odd since you're dealing with credit card debt (which affects your credit score) but if you take the time to close the accounts, it's likely to be more damaging than if you leave the debt at the very least for a bit longer.

The first thing you must do is begin to make payments. Even when you owe a large amount of cash to an credit card company, or a lender, they'll rarely close your account or turn the account over to a collection agency when you're paying them. They'll let you pay until you stop paying since it is at the very least, they expect to receive their full amount back. If they decide to sell your account off to a collection agency, they'll only receive one percent of the total amount due from the company. If you pay on time, you can improve your credit score as the algorithm used to calculate time payments doesn't take into account whether the amount due is due. It only considers whether the payment was received on time.

If you keep making timely payments, you also earn credit. If you're credit-worthy, this is also a benefit. If you shut down those accounts, you will lose the credit which means your credit rating is likely to decrease (even even though you've cleared yourself of the debt). Therefore, make sure that you keep those accounts open, and don't pay the debt due. Once you've gotten the balance down to a point which you are able to maintain, you will be able making purchases, and then pay them off. This will help improve your credit score even more quickly.

After you've paid the outstanding debt , your credit provider will not be able to take your credit card as swiftly since you'll have additional costs to pay, and they'll now have more confidence in your ability to repay them. They're likely to allow that you keep your card , and it will improve the likelihood of building credit. The open credit and having a lower minimum balance on your cards can boost your score many points.

A low balance is that you are careful not to use much cash on credit cards and keep the balance to a minimum. When you sign up for credit cards, you're provided with the option of a limit. It's the sum you can spend with that credit card. If you maintain the balance (the amount you've spent) in the lower end of the limit, it increases your score on credit. If it's very high, your credit score is likely to decrease. But , you don't have to be concerned about every credit card (though it's the most efficient method of doing it).

All your credit card balances are combined to calculate your balance. If you own three credit cards totalling $1,000, $1,500, and $500, your credit limit is $3000. If your credit card with a $500 limit is fully topped up however you haven't used any funds on any of the other credit cards, then the credit rating is likely to be quite excellent because your amount is around 16 percent of the credit you have available. If you'd maxed out your highest-priced card, the amount of credit utilized would be around 50%, which is not looking great on your credit score.

To improve your credit score, it is important to be aware of your balances. Make sure to reduce them and make sure to pay on them regularly. This will allow you to build an image of trustworthiness and it will also assure that other credit organizations are more than willing to grant you credit and allow you to keep the credit too. If possible, you should ensure that this occurs because the only way you can increase your credit score is having credit. Simply getting rid of the debt will not suffice.

Another thing to bear in your head is to cooperate with credit card companies as well as lending companies. If possible, you can, don't allow your accounts to be referred to a collection company. You'll pay more to a collection agency , and it's going to show less favorable on your credit record. It will also remain in your credit file for a long time longer than late payments made to the bank. If you're required to make many payments over a lengthy period of time, you'll benefit with this method.

In the end, if you don't have credit card accounts available, you should to acquire them. You should be able to have at minimum three cards with Revolving credit. This means that you should have three credit cards you use and make punctually payments for. If you can do this, it will help you improve your score while you attempt to fix any other issues. The new cards might need to be secured as the business isn't confident in your credit score and is convinced that you'll default on amount that might or may not be due to them.

You must ensure that you receive the credit. You can use credit cards that have security and make sure that you pay them in time. If you follow this advice, it will improve your credit score. You'll be amazed by how quickly positive ratings begin to appear too. Make sure to take advantage of them and continue building credit. We'll give you a bit more information on the best way to rid yourself of certain accounts that are negative in the coming chapters. We'll also discuss how to keep your credit solid once you've managed solve the issue.

Chapter 12: What's your Credit Score?

Some people's credit scores can be a terrifying beast that they must confront every time they need credit. Although they know that in some way, it is related to their creditworthiness, it's still scary or expensive to deal with their credit score. However, your credit score isn't as terrifying as it might seem and it can actually help in the same way it could hurt. The distinction between a good and bad credit isn't as straightforward as if you're accepted or denied; it is as well what rate of interest you're borrowing money at. Establishing solid credit habits is crucial in order that when you need credit, it won't be a frightening monster but rather a factor you will benefit from.

A Mindset of Credit Mind Set of Credit

If you're yet to file for bankruptcy or been in credit all of your life, putting yourself in an attitude of confidence is likely to boost your score and your financial situation no matter what appears like today. Although, if you declared Bankruptcy this morning, it could take a bit longer to appear.

The most effective way to establish the habit of credit is to envision yourself as on an "credit" eating plan. Like a diet that you adhere to, sticking to your long-term goals will bring you success. It's acceptable to cheat occasionally or even make an purchase there or there that you'd like. However, the problem comes when this is a constant thing, or the entire credit plan is thrown out the window. Just like eating a healthy diet, knowing the condition of your credit is currently will provide you with an estimate of the time it will take to improve. If you're stuck living with credit cards, take a seat and look at the numbers to see whether you can come up with the right budget to keep the balance moving in the proper direction. If you find an impossible way and you're not sure, it's time to call a debt consolidation firm to help you get your credit back in order. They're in a unique position because they typically can get lower rates of interest through agreements that they negotiate with lenders. However beneficial consolidation services are, they could force you to close your credit cards and could have a negative impact on your credit score.

When many people think of credit , they imagine endless bills that drain their funds. Some are thinking of the many wonderful things they can get. What you need to know is that those with great credit may still be contemplating everything they'd like to purchase. But they are responsible and at a price which is not expensive. Let's suppose two people wish to purchase the same car the car is $10,000. The first one does not have a good credit score, and ends in paying $300 per month to pay for their car. The second one ends up paying only 150 dollars per month. This is a clear indication that the more bad your credit and the more expensive you're paying for interest, and the greater the cost. This can be applied to all credit related items including a mortgage to a credit card. I remember exactly when I switched on my utilities , they conducted an inquiry into my credit to see whether a deposit of 150 dollars was required. At the time , I was broke due to moving and was unable to be able to pay for the cost of the deposit. It's possible to say that 150 dollars isn't a lot however it's just one instance. All of these factors add up and the total might not always be that small.

How do you submit your application to get your initial credit card?

If you are considering applying, I'd recommend starting by contacting your banking institution, if it has one. Visit the branch and request to speak to someone from your bank regarding applying. They will be delighted to sit with you. However, before you sign anything, you must inform them of your credit score to help you determine a credit loan that will offers the greatest chances. A few of my first credit cards I was offered was one that was a "student" card, which was slightly more accommodating because it was specifically designed specifically for those with less credit background. Be careful as each credit card you apply for will be a subject of an inquiry on your credit report. If your application is approved, you're on the right track to excellent credit. If not, don't be concerned about it- today's businesses are more stingy than ever when it comes to credit. It is crucial to know the reasons you were rejected. The company won't just be required to provide you with an free report upon request but also provide the exact reasons for why it was rejected. Examine these reasons and determine if there's something you can improve the outcome before applying again. If you find that there's nothing that you could do to change further, then you could apply to a different firm. Also, do some research to determine which ones are most generous in their lending. Again, it's best to have three cards that you have balances that you can revolve, however, if you're brand new to credit, some credit background needs to be built before you can apply to get a loan.

The first card is delivered

The envelope is bent so that you feel the plastic card inside. It's there, shortly after, probably the credit card fever. Credit card fever happens the time when your credit card begins to transform into other items you'd like. It could be a brand new flat-screen TV or a record-breaking shopping record at the local shopping mall. Before using the card, even once it is essential to be aware of what you're entering into. Important things to consider on any credit card is the APR and limit. are. APR refers to the interest you be charged on any balance that is carried into the following month. Don't get discouraged if notice an APR of 30% staring at you, as with the right approach and discipline, it will decrease in time. The first step is to determine what the 40% of the total amount. Whatever this number comes out to be, should be your aim for the balance of the card. For example, if you have 500 dollars, then and spend 200 dollars with the card. From here , it's an issue of not making use of it until your balance is paid off a little. Therefore, wait until that bill in the next month, and then be ready to pay it. If you can, make an automatic payment via the credit card website. Feel free to make higher than your minimum amount but don't make a full payment to the amount. If a balance doesn't continue to carry from month to month doesn't exist in your credit report and could appear as a card that isn't being utilized. If it's the minimum amount or a double amount that you pay, it won't affect the score of your credit card directly.

What is the best time to consider applying for a different card?

This is a great question If you think your credit score is solid enough, then you are able to apply as soon as you are accepted for the first time. If you're doing very well with the first credit card, the bank could decide to increase the limit of your credit. This is a good indication that the company is deeming that you are less risky than they had previously. When your credit limit gets raised automatically, it doesn't make an inquiry in your credit report. If you haven't applied for a new card, a good time to do so is following the first automatic increase. I recommend using this method until you have at least three cards, based on the earlier guidelines for placing credit on each.

Contacting the credit card company

When you deal with your credit card company , there will be times where it's like tug of war. Because , in the end you're trying to stop your money out of their hands and they would like the reverse. When you are dealing with over limit or late charges, give them a phone call and see if they are able to reduce it. The majority of companies allow certain charges to be waived particularly for the first time. If you're not satisfied with that the interest rate is too high, should be reduced, inform them, the most they could do is to say no. If you've managed to keep a positive relationship with the business in the past, they'll be more inclined to cooperate with you.

Chapter 13: Your Credit Report

Are you curious about what your first step? It's easy, figure your current standing. I've coached many people with poor credit. I was even in poor credit, so I understand how frightening this process could be.

In the end, it's an issue to be aware in within your head that you've got a low credit score. It's very different to see the score in stark black or white screen. This is a scary thing and basically means that it is impossible to ignore the extent to which things are bad.

If you are able to take the risk it is actually releasing yourself from many anxiety in the near future. you may find that the situation isn't as bad as you think. There isn't any choice but to you must look over your report to determine what you can do to fix it.

Getting Your Credit Report

It's not difficult to access your credit report. In fact, you just need submit an application at the credit bureaus and you're entitled to one free credit report each year.

It is crucial to request your credit report from all three credit bureaus, Experian, Transunion, and Equifax since the reports differ from one bureau from the other. In essence, it is dependent on the credit union your providers are a part of. (The credit bureaus essentially blend the data received from different credit companies to produce your profile of payment as well as your FICO score.)

If you don't want to fill out applications for each website, there are sites that can do it for you. All you need to do is provide all the necessary information and they'll submit applications to credit bureaus on behalf of you.

Let's Take a Look at That Report

When you've got your report before you, you must take a look at it from a neutral perspective and pretend it's an anonymous report and they've been inquiring about lending the money. It is important to examine the report as though you were the lender rather than the borrower, and there will be some aspects you have to be aware of. Let's look at these in detail.

What kind of credit Do you have?

It's all about credit surely? It's true, but I must admit that this is something that astonished me when I found out about it. But, the kind of credit you take advantage of is an indicator of whether you're an honest lender or not.

The reality is that credit can be classified in two categories, installment credit and revolving credit. Revolving credit, similar to the type you receive with credit cards is a more flexible arrangement. If you're managing it correctly and paying the amount you should, you'll continue to have access to the maximum credit limit. This means that you can utilize all the money with no fees and the interest you pay to the credit card. It is possible that you will never be able to pay off the debt.

A contract for installment credit is not an open-ended contract at all. You choose the time you want to pay back your debt and you have to make monthly payments in accordance with the terms agreed upon. As the duration of the loan gets longer the amount of debt will be reduced, and generally, you won't be able to take that cash out again.

Which one do you think is more risky in the context of new possible lending institutions?

Your Credit History

Did you think that you could simply slide over the payment for the month that you paid or did not make it in a few days? The entire information you entered is stored in you payment records. Even if you pay your bills in a single day over the month, you'll be identified as a slow-payer.

It's something that many aren't aware of that is the importance of making sure you pay your bills in time every month. Your history of payments is one of the aspects that potential creditors will carefully examine because your past actions are the most reliable indicator of what to expect in the future. If you've had a long streak of late payments it gives the impression that you're not able to meet the costs of the current amount of debt or that you're irresponsible in the way of paying bills . In either case it's a negative image of the creditor.

It is also important to keep in mind that even though the FICO score is based on the most recent six months into consideration the full history of your payments for each account remains displayed. Therefore, you have to remain consistent with your efforts and continue to maintain your excellent behavior because anyone who checks your credit score will view the entire payment history.

How much debt you could be able to

This is yet another aspect that many people don't realize makes an impact. Let's say you're a prudent borrower and you never use up your credit cards to the max - how much are the credit limit? A prospective creditor has to evaluate the overall amount of debt you could be able to take advantage of - perhaps today you've not yet used your limit for store cards, but there's no reason to stop you from using it in the future.

If you had only spent $500 on four of your credit cards, your balance could, for instance increase by $2000 in a matter of seconds and your payment profile could be different too.

How many accounts you have

Credit is a fickle nanny It is essential to have a few accounts you have to pay to prove that you're creditworthy. After you've proven that you're creditworthy, it's likely that everyone would like to offer you credit. The issue of having multiple credit accounts from a lender's perspective isn't just that you are at a greater risk of likelihood of exposure.

It could also be seen as an indication that you're in financial trouble. What is the reason you have three credit cards as well as five store cards if you're so proficient in managing your finances?

How much do you actually Owe?

This is a major ore evidently, but there are several diverse things to take into consideration in this regard.

The first thing to consider is how much are you overall exposure to debt, and how does it affect the ability of you to repay it? Creditors are looking to know that you're able to manage the debt you have, but that you are able to handle the debt you're trying to get.

Repayments on debt, including mortgage debt, must be at least 30percent of your monthly income - after deductions. Your mortgage shouldn't be more than 30% of the total monthly income after deductions.

The most important thing for creditors, however, is how you make use of the credit you already have. This is where that the majority of people fall short in the gap between their excellent credit rating and the average or fair one.

Consider it for one second If your friend exhausted all their credit cards and taken out loans all over and still came back to you to take out the loan Would you be delighted to lend the money to them?

Incessantly exceeding your credit limit, particularly when they are revolving credit limits, is a clear indicator of either one or two conditions - either are in debt more than you are able to handle and you need to take advantage of credits to boost your earnings, or you're not responsible in your spending habits. If you wish to be into the high-end category with regards to scoring your FICO, then you should not use more than 30 percent of your credit limit at any time. (does do not include mortgage limit)

Chapter 14: Your Credit Report

If you're planning to obtain another card with a credit limit, buy an important asset with a mortgage, or apply for new utility connections, or search for new employment You should be aware that your credit score can be either your greatest partner or your the worst foe. Why? The reason is that your credit history, which is prepared by at most one major agency or credit bureau which your creditors provide all of your credit data, informs financial institutions, prospective employers, as well as utility firms about your financial risk. Furthermore, your financial risk influence the decision of which of them to engage you, provide you with an extension of credit or grant the access you need to utility services. Also, considering that the credit report or other information contained therein are essential to the calculation of your credit score, looking for any errors and being able to challenge and rectify them will assist in improving your credit score, too.

Examine for possible errors in Your Reports

Credit reports are created by individuals using data gathered from people. Since humans are human as well, and no human is perfect, it's possible for credit reports to be contaminated with errors. The errors could differ in their nature and severity in the form of timely payments that weren't recorded to bankruptcy applications that were incorrectly reported that could show up in your credit reports, and harm the credit rating.

Because your credit score can affect the most important things you do like job searching or applying for utility connections, or borrowing money, it is important to be sure that your credit reports accurately portray the financial status of your business. Undiscovered errors can put you at chance of damaging your reputation for your financial standing.

In many countries, including those of the United States, the law gives borrowers the right to complete credit scores. Thus credit bureaus are forbidden from filing incomplete, unsubstantiated or incorrect credit reports. In these states, the law gives that borrowers just like you have the right to challenge inaccurate information and numbers that appear on your credit report , which originate from credit bureaus and request their removal or correction to your credit reports.

How do you determine whether the credit reports credit bureaus produce about you are correct? The first step is to obtain a copies of your credit reports which you can obtain by a variety of methods. One is to obtain a free copy through major credit report websites such as www.AnnualCreditReport.com. Another option is to ask for the free version of your credit history from the credit bureaus. This is your right under specific circumstances of certain regions, including in the United States:

* You're the recipient of welfare or assistance from the government;

* You're seeking work but are not employed;

* You've recently been a person who was the victim of identity theft or
* Your application for credit, job or utility connection application was rejected due to negative information in your credit report, as well as your poor credit scores.

In certain areas of some areas of the United States, the law provides you with a free credit report each year. This is in addition to those free credit reports you're entitled to get through other sources.

If the free credit report isn't offered in your state You can purchase your own copy from the top credit bureaus. How much? It is dependent upon the bureau that you are dealing with,, but typically, credit reports cost between $10 and $20 for a copy. If you receive reports from various credit agencies or bureaus You must be sure that you compare them with one another because they might contain different errors.

Once you've got your copy, go through every item in detail. You must have essential financial documents, such as statement of accounts, billing statements and official receipts that prove standing-by payments. These documents are your evidence or to help you dispute incorrect items that appear on credit reports.

Disputable Errors

If you're looking for mistakes, you are able to almost certainly contest all types of mistakes on the credit reports. A mistake is an error, no matter the extent, size or impact to your credit score. You are entitled to a complete credit report that's as secure as your freedom to breathe or drink. However, while you are able to dispute any information in your report Credit bureaus aren't required to examine and correct every one of them under the laws which are in force in their respective jurisdictions.

What are the items in your credit report you can contest and make credit bureaus to rectify or remove to your advantage? You can generally contest items on your credit report that cannot be independently verified and that are incomplete, out of date and incorrect. Incorrect information can include negative information like bankruptcy, for example. These will only appear visible on your credit reports for a short duration. If you're in the United States, bankruptcy can be reported in your credit report for up to 10 years, while other negative information will only appear visible for a maximum of seven years. If your credit report contains your bankruptcy date of fifteen years back, then you are able to contest the report and demand the credit bureau who prepared your report to eliminate it from both your prospective and current credit reports.

What are the other inaccurate information on your credit file you could challenge? They include:

Balances or accounts that aren't yours;

Incorrect balances on accounts and credit limits

* Erroneous creditors;

Incorrectly reported statuses for the accounts e.g. the account is current, but it's reported to be due; or

* Timely payments were reported incorrectly as late.

The Dispute

After you have identified any errors on your credit reports, which can be challenged by the credit bureaus who created them, you are able to pick between two options for disputing them: via snail mail or via the Internet.

It's the Snail Mail Dispute

The process of disputing mistakes by mail could take quite a bit of time. Therefore, why would you look at snail mail as an option to contest mistakes on the report on your credit? Two words paper trail. This could prove particularly beneficial if, for any reason your credit bureau's reply to your dispute is not timely.

In discussing response times or turnaround times for disputes the credit bureaus are required to conclude their investigation and respond within 30 days after the dispute was submitted. The time frame for response can extend to up to 45 days provided you submit additional documents to back up your claim following the bureau's investigation been initiated. The United States, the law provides you with the right to sue the bureau in question for as much as a million dollars in the event that they don't respond within the specified time.

If you decide to submit an appeal by mail, make sure you write in a way that clearly mentions the details that need to be removed or changed and the reason that the information is not accurate or no longer relevant. Include any documentary evidences to can support your claim, like statements of accounts and official receipts that prove the actual amount of money paid, among other things.

When you mail your dispute letter along with copies of the documentary evidences send them via registered mail. This way you'll have a reliable and unquestioned proof that you submitted - and that they accepted - your complaint on a particular date on when the 30 or 45 day time frame will be determined. While you wait for the credit bureau's response ensure that you keep your eye on the processing time to ensure that you make sure you send them timely reminders.

The Online Dispute

If you're looking for convenience it's hard to beat making your complaints online. You can do it at sitting at your own home and at the best time. More than the ease of making a dispute online it is also possible to determine the status of your dispute and see the outcome online as well. What's not to like?

These conveniences and comforts come with some challenges to overcome however. One of these is that you'll have to mail your document evidence via postal mail. This means that you'll need to visit Post Office, your nearest mailbox, or to the closest courier service in order to mail tangible documents directly to the credit bureau.

Another issue you'll have confront in the event that you decide to submit your dispute online is that you'll only be able to see the outcomes of the bureau's investigation and analysis of your filed complaints online, i.e., you will not receive a physical copy of the report from them. This could be a problem when you're required to show evidence of the fact that your credit file that was used by an lender, bank or utility company which has recently refused to accept your application is a false one.

The Process

When you submit a dispute claim at the credit bureau that compiled the incorrect credit report, they will respond in various ways. They can respond immediately by amending or deleting the information that you contest. However, if the credit bureau is in a position to confirm the disputable information later do not be shocked to see the information reinstated on your credit reports. If the bureau does this, they're required by the law to inform the person who reinstated you in writing.

As previously mentioned the credit bureaus are typically required by law to resolve dispute on credit reports within a maximum period of 30 days from the time of receiving the dispute. This period may be extended to 45 days if further evidence to back claims is filed after investigations have been conducted. After the completion of investigations credit bureaus are required to inform those who have filed disputes with the findings that they have uncovered during their research. They may even provide free copies of updated credit reports when the disputes are verified and reported in the credit reports. Additionally the credit bureaus could be required to send formal notices of corrections and/or amendments in credit records to organizations which rely on these erroneous reports to decide against applications submitted to these institutions.

Third Party Error

It's possible that the mistake on your credit report was not the error of the bureau but rather the source of the information, like the bank that you have an outstanding balance on your loan with, or the credit card company you use. If the response from the credit bureau to your complaint states that your error was confirmed by the credit card company or your bank company, it's the best option to contact the relevant institution and submit the dispute directly to them instead.

Others Erroneous Credit Reports

In the event that your credit reports from a particular credit bureau turns out to be inaccurate it's likely you're credit records from different bureaus may be incorrect. Why? It's because they all receive all the information they require from the same source, i.e., your creditors. Therefore, it will it be within your interest to ensure that the credit reports of other bureaus are reliable and free of errors, too.

Documentary Evidence to Back Your Disputes

If you contest certain bits of information from your credit report to the credit bureau who created it you'll have to show that the responsibility falls on you. You'll need to show the existence of this information is not correct and shouldn't be included on your credit report. As with the court case, you'll require documents to support your claims.

If the dispute is related to your personal information , such like name, age birthday, date of birth, or your social security numbers, the primary documentary evidences to file a dispute are the originals of your valid identification documents and documents proving your birth certificate or marriage certificate, as well as the most recent statements of your billing. If the issue is about the alleged "missed" payments or checks that have been cancelled, copies of the check or official receipts that prove payments, or most recent statements of accounts showing the existence of "missed" payments need to be provided to your credit agency with your official request for a letter. Make sure to send duplicates of your original documentation but not the originals, which must be kept on your desk always.

As we mentioned that you should anticipate a more lengthy response time of up to 45 days when you submit additional documents following the time that the credit bureau began to investigate your dispute. If you provide all documents in support of your complaint, the most amount of days for which the credit bureau has to reply to you is just 30 days.

Chapter 15: Avoiding Getting Your Credit Report Since It will affect Your Credit Score

The truth about the frequency and quantity of credit inquires that are conducted only make up 10 percent of the credit rating. Contrary to what many believe it is not a problem to the credit rating of yours by making inquiries on your own credit. You can check your credit report each day for two months , and your score won't be affected.

It's true that excessive LENDER inquiries could affect your score on credit. But the frequency at which you review your credit report will have little effect upon your rating. In your credit report, it will be listed as an "Soft Inquiry" and will not affect your score. It is important to note that the Credit Bureaus are well aware that you have to and should be keeping an eye on your credit. Therefore, they view checking your credit report an act of responsible conduct. Make sure you do it regularly and frequently. It is recommended to check your credit report at least every 6 months. It is required by the Fair Credit Reporting Act (FCRA) obliges each of the three nationwide consumer reporting agencies (Equifax, Experian, and TransUnion) to give you an free copies of the credit report upon request, every 12 months. So, make use of this opportunity. Be sure to purchase an FICO credit score at the company that will give you the exact score that lenders be able to see. Visit www.myfico.com to buy the credit score.

Applying for or being a joint Credit with your spouse

The idea of applying for or having joint credit is not a good approach and is a huge error. Not only because of the potential issues that could arise from divorce, but due to the fact that married couples can make use of each their credit. Simply by making plans and ensuring separate credit accounts, their credit will become an important aspect in financial concerns.

If you think about the issue of the joint loan from a risk management standpoint you're potentially exposing yourself to the behavior of your spouse. This can be a particular issue during divorce. From a strategic standpoint it is possible to establish separate credit. This can provide a significant boost to the finances of a couple. If you're married and you have managed your credit on your own, you may make use of your spouse's credit when it becomes important. For instance, if you require a line of credit, but there is a large utilization (high amount) on the credit card you have and you want to transfer the position of the balance to the credit cards of your spouse. You can now walk into the credit union or bank to apply for the loan with a low personal credit and a better than average credit score. You can basically reduce your spouse's credit score in order to secure an interest rate that is better. This is just one of the ways to leverage your own credit.

Don't check for errors on your Credit Report

Do you believe that 80percent of people have an error of a certain kind on their credit report? Yes with 25% of these mistakes being so serious that they could cause the denial of loans, mortgages or jobs. Recent Federal Reserve Board study of more than 300,000 consumer credit reports revealed that 46% had at the very least one credit limit. This can be a huge slap to one's credit score.

The biggest errors you could commit is believing your credit report is correct. It is likely that you'll have at most one error in your report. If you don't currently have one it is likely to happen in the near future.

There are many mistakes that aren't important; however, by promptly rectifying them, you can significantly improve the credit rating of your client. Correction of errors can be extremely long and time-consuming however the reward is worthwhile. When you prioritize the errors based on their impact on your score on credit, you'll improve your credit score in the fastest method possible as you rectify them. This means you will benefit the most quickly. Next, you can tackle the less important ones that have little or no impact on your score but must be rectified.

High-priority errors can reduce the credit rating by 50 to 100 points. These are:

* Collections Accounts

The incorrect credit limit is not being applied.

The address is incorrect. Security Number or Address

* Incorrect Bankruptcy debt discharged reporting

If you have the correct kind and amount of Credit Cards While keeping the right balance of debt in relation to your credit limit every month will boost your credit score substantially. Eliminating High Priority errors from your credit report will increase your credit score significantly. Even having an Bankruptcy appearing on your report.

There is no plan to improve your credit score

In only a glance your credit score could be affected dramatically. Creditors are constantly reporting to the credit bureaus. they can also add the possibility of identity theft which means your score could be wiped out in a flash. Therefore, you must develop a strategy for maintaining your score. In the absence of a strategy, is one of the biggest errors you can make.

* Prepare an account of your budget

• Be thrifty if currently in financial trouble Make use of technology to keep and improve the credit score of your. Be sure to check your monthly credit card statements and bank statements. your credit report each six months

* Always use the exact as the name you used when applying to credit

* Make sure your accounts are active.

Make sure you protect your credit prior to and after divorce. improve your credit score to at minimum 720.

The quickest way to improve your Credit

A majority of people don't see credit as crucial in their early times. Many believe, "I'm not ready to purchase a home and what's the issue?" Just because you're not in a position to purchase a home doesn't mean you don't need credit. Be aware that certain employers won't hire people with poor credit scores. Poor credit score people pay higher rates of interest on credit cards and auto loans. In fact, auto insurance premiums in some states are more expensive for those with poor credit scores. Landlords aren't ready to approve applications from those with low credit scores. Therefore, trying to build your credit is not a good idea.

The more serious an individual's credit troubles is, the greater the chance that to recover from the financial strain that leads to it, and the subsequent credit blemishes that can occur when different circumstances occur.

It is equally important that teenagers begin to establish their credit when they are still at the house with their parents. So, once they leave the home, they will be well prepared for the world of credit, which only accepts them as a three-digit number. It can be as easy as having a joint credit card for siblings and parents and the control of the card held by from the parent.

Don't Pay Attention to Your Credit All Together

There are many who have bankruptcies and repossessions or any other serious delinquencies, and they are unable to access credit at all. One of the worst things you can do to your credit score is to wash off the mess. Remember my earlier statement that the credit score is not as important as a poor credit. In the near future, you'll require credit. If you are a citizen who is cash-only you'll prolong the time your credit score isn't high enough to qualify for great rate of interest, loan or credit conditions.

If you have bad credit, or have no credit, you could and should apply for credit as soon as possible regardless of whether you've been through bankruptcy. You may apply for secured credit cards and this is one you need to make on deposit, which is usually $300. The card will typically have an upper limit of $300 but if you make use of it in a responsible manner it will cause your score to rise. It is recommended to aim for the elusive score of 720 credits which you could achieve within 2 to 5 years If you adhere to these easy guidelines.

Chapter 16: Understanding The Laws

A lot of mistakes can be made because you don't understand the rules that are part of The Fair Credit Reporting Act (FCRA) as well as your state's laws regarding credit reporting.

FCRA was passed on the 26th of October in 1970, allowing consumers to increase the accuracy of their credit reports by giving them the chance to dispute and rectify negative information. This is an extremely valuable tool. There's so much information available regarding this subject but, unfortunately, I'll be able to draw attention to just a few. If you would like to review a complete copy of the Fair Credit Reporting Act go to: http://www.ftc.gov/os/statutes/fcradoc.pdf

Furthermore, laws can differ between states, and it is crucial to study the specifics of your state prior to submitting any complaints in the state bureaus. For the majority of states the information you need is available through your state's Secretary of State's website.

If you are looking for quick fixes to your credit report there are some things to think about

"Statue of Limitations- This is one of the most effective methods of getting the old debts deleted from the credit file. In accordance with the FCRA If a debt is not paid in seven years of its initial date of insolvency, it will be deleted from your credit report. Many states have a statue of limitations which is typically smaller than that of the Federal statue. In my state, there is a 3 year statute of limitation. It is crucial to know the fact that Federal law will override State law. However, usually credit bureaus remove the collection in dispute after a written notice informing them of the statue of limitation for the State is received.

*Duplications This is a fantastic illustration of how you can get rid of this section on your credit report quickly. FCRA was enacted to ensure that information provided to the Bureaus is true. In many

cases, those who have many collections on their credit report may notice multiple collections. This occurs when a creditor attempts to collect the debt but cannot collect. The debt is then sold to a collection agency for pennies per cent. After that, it is reported back for the Bureaus as an entirely new collection. It is not uncommon for an item to be sold five or six times. This is a problem of accuracy. The reason for this is because the previous collector reported this debt with a zero balance. Since the collector prior to the dispute does not hold this collection, that debt is not valid anymore. It's as simple as that ... In the event that you don't owe any business a debt that appears on your credit record the company is not permitted to report you as owing the balance, and you may contest the credit.

*Licensing - This is another of my top techniques. This will require some research on your part, but it must remain among the first things you consider in order to have an obligation canceled. There are many companies that do not have a legal business licenses. It sounds crazy, but it's the truth! On the Secretary of State of your state's website, you should be able search the databases of business entities as it is public information. If the company isn't authorized in the state you reside or their license is expired, there's an opportunity to remove the information from your records.

*Debt Validation is the process where an entity, who has an obligation, must demonstrate to you that it's actually your debt. Fortunately, for you and I as consumers, this can prove to be rather difficult for the company because their bookkeeping/accounting skills may not be totally accurate. If a debt has been transferred multiple times, the chances are greater that they'll not be able to provide you with precise details. If they can't demonstrate it...then they'll need remove the debt! !

If they can show that they are able to, then it is essential to look for any contradictions and then file an appeal for inaccurate data on your report. I've encountered cases in which debt validation was our last resort . When we received the data from the collection firm and analyzed the data, we discovered that the day of collection had been seven years back. The collection company did not realize that they had actually provided the information required to get the collection taken off in accordance with the statute of limitations.

Chapter 17: Student Loans explained

The purpose of a student loan is to assist students in paying for trade school or university tuition along with books, costs of living. It could differ from other kinds loan in the sense that its interest rate could be significantly lower, and the repayment plan could be delayed while the student is in school , but then paid back after the course is completed.

The United States, there are two kinds that student loans are federal ones that are sponsored by federal governments, and private student loans. This generally includes state-affiliated non-profits as well as institution loans offered by institutes and schools.

Federal student loans

The Federal Student Loans are accessible via the Federal Perkins Loan Program or the Federal Direct Loan Program. Parents and guardians can borrow cash at a low rate of interest straight from federal officials. The borrower should research federal loans prior to the use of private loans for students.

Federal Perkins Loans are low-interest loans available to students in the undergraduate and graduate levels with exceptional financial needs. There is no charge for interest for students who are at least half-time in their education There is also a grace period of nine months prior to when repayment begins once term ends. Federal Perkins Loans are not available in all schools. Check with the school's financial aid office to find out if they participate with the loan program.

Directly subsidized loan are those that are that are governed by federal regulations and only available to students who have demonstrated financial need. Direct subsidized loans have no interest if students are at least half-time in the classroom and is deferred for an amount of time when loans are delayed.

Unsubsidized federal loans differ than direct loans that are subsidized since they do not have to be based on needs. The school decides how much you are able to borrow in accordance with the cost of your attendance, in addition to any other financial aid that you receive. The interest is charged throughout all times and capitalized. Capitalization is charged while you are in school as well as during the grace period following graduation when payments are due and deferment period.

Direct PLUS Loans, also known as PLUS loans are a way to students pay for expenses related to education in the amount of tuition, however all other financial aid is taken out of the equation. These are unsubsidized federal loans for the parents of dependent students and for graduate/professional students who qualify. In any time and will be capitalized, therefore those borrowing should take into account this fact.

Students must look into grants, scholarships and federal student loans as a way to boost savings before deciding to take out the possibility of a private student loan.

Private Student Loans

The private student loan is credit-based loans. The loan's leaders will look over your credit score, your capability and willingness to repay to be eligible for the loan as well as your interest rate. Private loans offer diverse payment options. This might include making payments during the school. This could help lower your interest rate and the overall cost of loan.

Students' loans must be repaid regardless of whether you finish your education. Insolvency on a student loan can be a huge blow to your credit score and hinder your chances of getting a car loan, credit card, mortgage or even get a job. This could lead to lawsuits against you, which could cost you a large amount of money.

Federal vs. Private Student Loans

Governments across the country offer two programs under two programs: the Federal Perkins Loan Program and the Federal Direct Loan Program and certain loans are offered regardless of financial needs. If parents/guardians or students are in search of loans, they should think about federal loans prior to considering privately-funded student loans. The federal government is able to offer students loans with a favorable interest rate. They also come with benefits, including the option of paying with a variety of options and advantages that private student loans aren't required to offer. Federal loans are "subsidized" as well as "unsubsidized." This means that interest does not accrue on loans that are subsidized while students are at the school. Students' loans can also be part of a financial aid package which could include scholarships, grants or work study programs that could make college more affordable.

After you have explored your options for federal student loans, you may want to consider the possibility of a private student loan as an alternative option. These loans are provided by credit unions, banks as well as others private lending institutions. The private student loan is based on creditworthiness which means that your credit score is the most important factor for interest rates and acceptance of the loans. Contrary to federal student loans, private student loans often are characterized by variable interest rates, which may increase after completion.

Federal Student Loans are a huge business
Student loans from the federal government are more costly than private student loans, but Don't fall for the rumor that the earnings of government. The profits for US government are worth the risk. Prior to the year 2010 federal loans were split into direct loans that were financed with federal funds, and private student loans, also known as guaranteed loans, which were held by private lenders, but backed by the federal government. The federal government saw the benefits from the guarantee lending scheme and decided to take over the lending industry, removing the guarantee lending program in. The federal student loan program earns billions of dollars in profits for the government as the interest payment is higher than expenses for borrowing, loan

losses and administrative expenses that are incurred by government agencies like the US government.

The federal government's losses in student loans is incredibly low due to the laws the US government enacted to collect federal student loans differ from the majority of other loans in America. Students cannot discharge their loans in bankruptcy unless the repayment of the loan will cause the possibility of "undue difficulty" for the borrower and their dependents. This is a unique situation due to the fact that IRS Tax debts are subject to bankruptcy. The majority of other debts require a legal process prior to wage garnishment however this isn't the case for student loans.

The majority of college students in the United States qualify for federal student loans, regardless of their family's financial status and credit history. The only exceptions are those who have defaulted on federal loans or were convicted of drug-related offenses and who have not completed a rehabilitation program , so they are left wide open for young Americans to fall into debt prior to obtaining their first job in the modern slavery.

.

Chapter 18: Credit & Credit Reports

How do you define credit?

In a more concrete instance, let's say you borrowed money from a friend or you requested her to take care of your children and you promise to pay her back at the end of the month or at an agreed date, or, if you don't have the funds to pay for the product or service you require and you have promised the person who you purchase with that you'll pay them by a particular date, that's credit. It's basically borrowing the item or service now, and paying it back later in the form of money. A few years ago, retailers would let their customers, or, primarily, those they are familiar with, to shop for food items and then pay on a specific date, such as their pay day, for instance and then they would store the information into their own credit accounts. If the customer is able to pay the payment before or on the scheduled date, the store owner may allow the customer to purchase more products from the shop since the store is confident that the customer will be able to pay. If, however, you're not able to make the payment on time, or you did not settle the bill, you may not be permitted to make credit on the items in the future. The retailer could use this information to notify other retailers about the incident that impacted your credit and this could affect the way they permit you to make an order for credit.

These days, stores have grown larger, and are owned by high-end and large businesses and corporations that accept the payment of cash, checks or credit card. As time passes businesses are becoming more sophisticated and are more cautious when lending money, goods or services to individuals to ensure they don't get ripped off. This is why certain security measures such as the background check and credit score are set in the system. This ensures that consumers are able to pay the amount they are owed.

A Short History of Credit Reporting

Over a 100 years ago when supermarkets were merely small stands manned by an individual in the family who runs the business of a small size credit of any kind was practiced. Just like modest beginning, these tiny retailers bonded with other merchants and discussed their customer's profiles. They they began to trade customer's financial data with business owners in an organization of merchants. As time passes these organizations would become larger as more companies join and new organisations will emerge. The data that was written on paper was replaced by typescript or stored in folders until computers began to progressed and all information was made digital.

Retail Credit Company, predecessor of Equifax was the first in the process of collecting and selling consumer information to companies and organizations. It was established in 1899 by Atlanta commercialist Cator Woolford in 1899, and was the very first Credit Reporting Agency (CRA). The business of CRA was then growing slowly, but it was not until it gave birth to TransUnion in the latter half of the 60's.

A controversy erupted in the 60's regarding the credit reports issued by these firms. Between 2000 and 2006 Chris Hoofnagle was a senior counsellor at the Electronic Privacy Information Center (EPIC) according to his report the credit reports were used to decide whether to accept loans and other services. Consumers were not able to look at their credit scores prior to and the CRA's only reported negative information that was not needed about the person. The reports would contain information about the lifestyle, political views sexual orientation, other such things.

Due to this inconsistency among the CRA's, a significant congressional inquiry was conducted in 1971. FCRA also known as the Fair Credit Reporting Act was acknowledged by Congress. The inquiry resulted in a system that ensures accurate, reliable and safe credit report. The law promoted fair information procedures that safeguard a consumer's privacy and data, while allowing the consumer to review, rectify and challenge any incorrect details about their account.

In 2001, customers finally have directly access to their credit rating. The amended version , signed by the previous president George W. Bush in December 2003 required that CRAs provide consumers with a fair cost. Nowadays, there are numerous ways to access your credit scores. we'll give links in the end of this book.

What are credit scores?

If you think that you were getting scores aren't that different from those of when you were in school, you should think about it. As adults, your credit score are often the factor that can decide whether or not you are your chances of purchasing a brand new car or home.

The credit score is the primary element for credit unions and banks on whether they are willing to take on the risk of offering you loans or money. It's a 3 digit number calculated through a mathematical process based on the information contained in the credit reports of your customers. It's designed to predict the risk of your credit, and specifically, the possibility that you'll be in delinquency on your obligations to your credit in during the following 24 months.

In addition to being the basis for loans or credit card approval and credit scores, they are utilized by other companies and businesses for applications to jobs and other applications.

In determining your credit score using a specific method or formula for calculating your credit scores is employed in the process, which is is known in the field of Predictive Analytics. They make use of certain data and then analyze it to arrive at the conclusion of a consumer's credibility when it comes to the payment of debt, and whether they can handle more credit lines. The most frequently used method formula is one that was created in FICO, the Fair Isaac Co Company, which is now called FICO. Another source of credit scores is

VantageScore. We'll discuss these scores more in the future.

What is FICO?

FICO is the acronym as Fair Isaac Co, a company that offers the majority all credit score we are familiar with in the present. The company was founded in 1956 by engineer Bill Fair and its Mathematician Earl Isaac. They launched ASAP, their very first automated application-processing system that debuted in Wells Fargo bank in 1971. Nowadays, the word FICO does not only refer to the business however, it also refers to the mathematical formula they employ to calculate their analytics. Different analytical algorithms were designed to meet the different requirements of every company that seeks to obtain an applicant's or a consumer's credit score. FICO also calculates their scores on information collected by the three major credit bureaus that are Equifax, TransUnion and Experian and the data they've gathered, they apply a particular formula to determine the probability of an individual being able pay their credit on time, or even if they'll be bankruptcy in a short amount of after.

What is the basis of what makes up your FICO scores?

In general it is the FICO score range is 300 to 850, with the higher score means lower risk for the bank or guarantee. Customers with excellent FICO scores of 760 or higher will likely to receive the most favorable rates for borrowing less, pay lower interest, and get the most attractive discount on insurance.

This pie chart will show what is included in your FICO score.

* 10% is determined by the fact that it's the first time you've applied for credit, or the amount of inquiries have been made on your credit score. We'll talk more about credit inquiries in the future.

* 10 percent is determined by the type of accounts you've held

*15 percent is the average age that your credit score is. Your credit score is longer the more favorable

* 30% comes from the amount of the debt you have

161

The 35% figure is by far the biggest amount, and refers to your past payment history , if you have had any late payments or you always pay your bills in time

Each of these factors is additionally assessed in other credit score models, and so it is clear that if you've got an impressive solid FICO score, the odds of you achieving a high scores in different credit score models is very high. However, for some people the weighting of these categories could differ. For instance, individuals who haven't used credit for a long period will be regarded differently than those with a long credit history, as per FICO. Therefore, the importance of each of these aspects is determined by the information contained in the credit file.

After the changes made to the FCRA several years ago, any information that is not considered to be relevant to your credit score are not considered to be part of the FICO score. This includes your personal views such as political views, sexual orientation as well as your private information, such as medical records, addresses and even your age.

FICO offers a variety of model of credit scores. Certain models are specifically tailored to the type of loan the customer is seeking. If you're applying for a car loan for instance, your prospective lender might employ an FICO score model that gives substantial weight to your record of paying auto loan installments. Some models have been modified to meet the needs of FICO's clients.

In addition, FICO modernizes its common formulas periodically and the most recent one being the FICO 9 launch in 2014. Collection accounts that are paid for are not included in FICO 9 score, while medical collections have a less negative influence on score in comparison against other scoring systems as well as older FICO algorithm.

What is VantageScore?

Similar to FICO, VantageScore is another kind of scoring for your credit. It was established in 2006 as an agreement on a program that was negotiated by three of the major credit bureaus, Equifax, TransUnion and Experian. It is also regarded as the second most trusted credit scoring system following FICO.

The most current version of VantageScore that was released, VantageScore 3.0 launched in March 2013 not only provides scores to all users, but also assists around thirty to 35 million individuals who do not have a profile of credit that is comparable to other models, be it because they're first timers with credit or don't utilize credit very often.

What are the factors that determine what makes up your Vantagescore scores?

Similar to other credit scores Similar to other credit scores, your Vantage score is based on calculations that are based on information from credit bureausnot the amount of income, bank accounts or other assets to determine how likely you will pay off your debts monthly on time. Your score is affected by the fact that you have a habit of paying promptly, and keeping your credit balances at a low level with respect to your credit limit total as well as the time of your credit account and its diversity, and the number of inquiries you have on you credit records.

The simpleness and common perception of credit scores is frequently ruined by numerous errors in credit reporting that could cause issues with credit scoring, that's why it's imperative be sure to monitor your scores. There are a variety of ways to examine your credit score.

A quick comparison of scores that are generated by FICO and VantageScore

After your scoring method is completed with their mathematical calculations of your credibility, you will receive your individual 3-digit score. In the above image you will be able see the difference with FICO scoring and VantageScore points system.

Rating FICO VANTAGESCORE

Extraordinary Excellent 800-850 775 and 800

Very Good/Good 740 - 700 749

Good / Fair 670 - 739 650 - 699

Fair / Poor 580 – 669 580 - 669

A Very Bad 300 579300 - 549

I'm able to say that when compared to FICO scores Vantage provides extreme and extreme scores. The range of scores provide on the Good and Poor fields are a little more than FICO's. The larger range of Vantage however is the Poor field. However, for the FICO pie they are identical to each other.

It's not true that Vantage places more weight to negative scores so that the applicant for a loan or credit card could be denied due to the variety of scores they offer. However, it's reasonable to conclude that the scores aren't entirely accurate. there are still a few ambiguities which you are able to dispute and rectify should the need arise.

Chapter 19: How To Establish Your

Credit

If you've never sought an loan or credit card before the procedure to get these types of financial security might be strange to you. Many people do not know where to start when it comes to how to go about the benefits of credit cards. The first step is to know that there's the need to conduct research prior to applying for credit card. Credit score can be the most crucial aspect when you apply for a credit card since there are a variety of credit cards that won't accept applicants with credit scores that are below an amount. For instance, certain fancy American Express credit cards require you to be able to pay an annual cost to access their services and the customers have to have credit scores that range from 750 to 850.

This is why in the beginning, when beginning to establish credit, it is important to make an application to credit cards generally referred to as "beginner" card. These cards are designed to accommodate people with less credit scores. One great instance of a line targeted at people who are just beginning to build credit score is that of the Discover It card. You should look into this kind of card if the opening of your account through Discover might help you with your credit-building goals. If you're not able to establish any credit whatsoever You may not be eligible for a card that is a starter card like Discover It. Don't panic. There are alternatives for people with no credit in order to improve their credit score. If there weren't any options for people who were just beginning, how could anyone improve their credit score? This article will discuss the steps to take in order to transform your credit from a nonexistent state to something reliable and stable.

Step 1. Make an application for a secured credit card

The only thing that makes secured and unsecure credit card differs is one thing: a secure credit card needs an upfront payment. The amount of the down payment required for a secured card is between three hundred and 500 dollars. This could explain why it is called a "secured" credit card because the cash you pay is an insurance policy for the credit. If you offer the credit company an amount of money to pay down in exchange for a promise that you will pay back the loan amount in the event that you fail to do so, as you'll forfeit the funds that you initially offered them. The activity you do with this card will help increase your credit score, so you make your payments in time obviously. Be careful not to confuse the debit card with secured credit cards. The history of your debit card is not recorded in your credit report.

Step 2: Charge Only That Can be Repaid Fully

It's best to begin with a small amount when you're first creating your credit. Alongside this it's also a smart decision to only make payments via your credit card when you are certain that you'll be able pay this cash back in full at the close each month. The principal way credit card companies earn cash is by paying interest every month on money borrowed that remains in your bank account as of the close each month. For instance, if you only purchase one pair of shoes using your credit card in the month, and they cost $75.00 It would be beneficial paying the company that issued your credit card in full $75.00 at the at the end in the current month. Of course, you'll are able to choose between paying $30.00 or any else amount you'd like to pay, however the rest of your money will accrue interest to it in the next month. This means you'll pay over $75.00 for shoes. If you are able to prove to lenders that you have the ability to manage debt, you'll be in good shape.

Step 3. Pay on time each month

Next, ensure that you pay your bills on the same date each month. It's pretty simple to explain. In the beginning, a single payment made with a credit card that is secured could be a big problem in the end.

Step 4: Review Your Credit Score

In the following six months you should check your credit score and check to obtain a credit report through your lender to confirm that there aren't any negative elements on it. If you find something that is negative, it can give you an understanding of what you could do much better next time around. A complete credit report will provide you with details about the number of credit lines you have open, as well as who has asked to review the credit reports of others, as well as it will also contain public records such as bankruptcies, foreclosures, and other issues that affect your credit score overall. This information will give you an excellent insights into the way your credit is used and the way your activities contribute in your credit rating all.

Step 5 5. Apply for an unsecured Credit Card

After one year of making purchases on a credit card that requires an additional security deposit, you ought to consider opening a credit card that is unsecured which means that the credit card doesn't require a down amount to pay. It is recommended to wait at least one year before you take this step because you'll need to allow your secured credit card the time to grow and establish your credit score first. It is also important not to apply for multiple credit cards with no security when you're ready to take the step.Each each time that you try to apply for the new credit card your credit score will decrease in a tiny way. It's not a good idea to decrease your credit score simply to apply for several credit cards in one go.

The most important thing to remember when trying to get credit even if there is none in the beginning is patience. It takes a lot of time for you to become a trustworthy and trustworthy borrower, but the advantages of having a good credit score are worth the effort essential. You'll save a huge sum of cash by developing your credit as early as possible in your life. It's well worth the time you pay for credit cards with no security to achieve this objective.

Chapter 20: Understanding Your Credit Report

The credit report you receive isn't very easy to comprehend. There are many various categories on your report, which means that you have to consider the various aspects to be sure you have a credit score that will be sufficient to obtain the items you desire.

The highest scores are those above 900, but few people actually get this. If you score greater than 700, then you have excellent credit and are almost guaranteed to get any kind of credit you could be eligible for. However, you should be aware that various types of credit card companies and agencies may require an individua score.

If your credit score is within the 600's, you're likely of being approved in most places, but not every. However, this isn't a guarantee. There are a lot of agencies who will take to be a tiny risk.

Credit score an indication of how high of a chance there is to lend you credit. When you first begin receiving credit, you will have an inadequate credit score. This informs the person looking at your score that there's the risk of high that is involved. They aren't sure if you'll be able to pay your bills or if you'll accrue a large amount of expenses. This is the reason your score is low. When you make more recorded payments, your score will go up as the probability of you not being able to pay things is decreasing.

There are a lot of other factors than payment delays or missed payments that could be a negative factor the credit rating. There are lots of other factors that can affect the credit rating (or raise it)

Let's take them apart and examine the information on your credit report.

Public records are among the first items that are listed when you check your credit score. The worst thing you could have judgments, tax liens and other infringements against you. All of them are likely cause a major slash in your credit score , and they'll affect you for a long period of period of time (up to seven years). Don't take to be a victim of these, if you can avoid to avoid it.

The next step is going come down to your financial accounts. This includes credit loans, cards or mortgages as well as any other credit accounts has been in use before. The majority of accounts considered older (closed longer than 10 years in the past) won't be reported unless you've had a collections of that account.

Each credit item will be reflected in the score of your credit. Every payment that is made on time will be counted in your favor , and each late payment, late payment or collection will be counted against you. Every balance will be reported, and excessive balances are likely to be a factor against you.

Remember that we mentioned earlier that you should have a good credit balance, but you also desire a lower debt on the credit card you're using. The way the credit reporting agency does is examine the amount you can spend on all your credit cards, and then add it all up. This is your credit balance. They will then calculate how much you have on each of these credit cards and add them total.

The amount due can be divided in half by the total available and you get your overall balance percentage. It is important to reduce this percentage as it will reflect positively on your credit score. A high percentage will cause your credit card make you look unprofessional and will reduce your credit score.

The total number of accounts you own along with the various types of accounts will contribute to your score, too. You should have a decent amount of account (more than 10) in order to ensure that you keep them up-to-date. Also, you should keep a variety different accounts (credit cards as well as mortgages, car loan and student loans, etc.) this will help boost your score.

In the end, the amount of questions you ask can affect your score. You should decrease the number of inquiries you make since each one of them will be a small ding on your credit report. The way they work is each time you make an application for credit. When you apply, they will check your credit score, and when they review your credit score, it decreases a slightly. The inquiries remain at the top of your credit score for a certain time.

This is why you should request credit less often and only when you're certain you'll be able to be approved. The credit you get will increase your credit score more than it will hurt the application.

All in all, you must be aware of the following things regarding your credit score:

You may have multiple account (10 plus)

Maintain all accounts up-to-date.

Do not keep public records

There are a range of kinds of account (loans or credit cards)

Keep your available balance high

Maintain the balance at a minimum

Do not apply for credit unless it is absolutely necessary

Don't apply for credit until you're certain you'll be accepted

Disput accounts that aren't accurate

Pay any outstanding accounts and pay off any collections

When you complete these steps, you can ensure that your score rise in time. It'll take time, and you'll definitely have to work on it, but you'll be able bring your score to normal. When you've brought your score back to normal, you'll discover it's easier to eliminate the debt and start saving more effectively as well.

The reason why your credit score will influence this is because your credit score will have much to do with your ability to get approved on everything from credit cards to auto loans to mortgages. It is also a factor in the interest rates you're offered. When your score increases, you'll be eligible to apply for lower interest rates , which helps you to pay off the debt and avoid debt in the future. Being debt-free means that you'll have more money to save for your savings. This is a win all around.

Chapter 21: Paying bills

I began to pay ALL My Bills on Time

If feasible, to pay in full every month. I cannot stress enough how crucial this move was to me. It's possibly among the top crucial actions one can take to improve credit scores and to maintain a healthy credit score.

I'm talking about ALL kinds of bills like mortgage or rent gasoline bill, power and water cell phone cable or satellite internet, credit card and loans, doctor's bills tuition costs and more. I was sure to pay any bill or statement I received from any source that I received on time.

If I could not afford to pay them in time? It had to be cut down on my spending.

When I pay my bills punctually, I am able to avoid penalties and late charges which can save my hundreds in the long run. Late fees for the credit card bill could be as high as $35! It's a huge penalty for even being a day overdue on a bill.

One late payment on one of your monthly bills could decrease your FICO score substantially. According to myFICO that making the payments on time is among the most important factors that impact improving your score on credit.

The history of your payments is a factor that accounts for about 35 percent the score on your FICO!

A general rule, which I have used to avoid buying items that I can't afford to pay for in full when the bill arrives. A home purchase or auto loans can be an exception.

I needed reminders to ensure that I was paying my bills in time. I set up reminders on autopilot or automated payments for all bill. I seldom login to my accounts to pay for bills and I can't recall the last time I made a check to mail in my the bill. I save all bills and statements come in to one spot and check this area at least every week. Be sure to keep track of all the bills that arrive!

The credit cards I use are scheduled to be paid out of my paying in full every month. I am confident that my payments are never overdue, and I will never transfer balances to the next month , thus keeping my interest costs to a minimum.

I'm planning to add details about collections accounts, too. Accounts that have not been paid on time are forwarded to a collection company that will seek to recover the amount due. Collection agencies are employed to recover the maximum amount owed as is possible. They employ various tactics to deceive people into paying. The items that have been handed over to the collection agency are deemed to be a negative or derogatory item on credit reports and can lower the FICO score significantly.

The process of paying off debts that were transferred to a collection company is something that a few people aren't keen on doing and instead, they just ignore the accounts (and frequent calls from collectors).

My suggestion is to settle all collections accounts whenever you can. This is my personal experience:

Collections will remain on your credit file for seven years after they're expected to be deleted. In the event that they remain on your credit report for seven years, there is no guarantee that they'll be removed because one collection agency may deal with you to sell the account agency and after that, the collection item gets shown on your report, as a negative item.

It shouldn't happen, however it did. This has was my experience. In trying to contact the collection agency regarding the new date of delinquency can be a difficult task.

7 year (or even longer) is an extended time to wait to check if the negative item can be removed. If it's not it will remain at the top of your credit score for seven more years.

I wanted to prevent the energy loss. I contacted the collection agency and tried to devise an arrangement to pay off my debt. Sometimes, they will take a smaller payment as a payment in full, and then report the account as"charge off. "charge off." Although charge-offs are considered to be a negative mark on my credit report but the charge was cleared and I was in the process of gaining peace of mind and improved credit over the long term.

Do you remember the school loan my father been able to include in bankruptcy? It was placed into collections when the bankruptcy was overturned and then was added to my credit file as an unfavorable credit item.

I arranged for payment through the agency that collects my debts, and asked whether they could erase the account from my credit history. I explained the situation in a very polite manner, and the representative told me he'd look into what could be done. I didn't anticipate anything considering how collection agencies work however, the report was taken off my credit report due to the fact that I had been making monthly payments towards the amount. It is impossible to know what sort of arrangement is possible with collection agencies. Request what you want in a manner that is friendly and then see what transpires.

Conclusion

I hope that the book helped know the basics of credit, and the best way to resolve your credit. I hope that you're in a position to comprehend the different ways you can apply them and, of course, if you have to utilize these methods, I hope that you're successful in repairing your credit.

It is the next thing to do: test one or two of these strategies yourself.